D0118122

how to start a home-based

Graphic Design
Business

how to start a home-based

Graphic Design Business

Jim Smith with Lisa Polce

gpp®

Guilford, Connecticut

Interior spot art licensed by Shutterstock.com

Editorial director: Cynthia Hughes Cullen
Editor: Meredith Dias
Project editor: Lauren Szalkiewicz
Text design: Sheryl P. Kober
Layout: Justin Marciano

ISBN 978-0-7627-8482-0

Printed in the United States of America

10 9 8 7 6 5 4 3 2 1

Jim Smith

I dedicate this book to my wife, Cindy Smith. While I cowrote it, Cindy cheerfully listened to me drone on about whatever chapter I happened to be working on and has acted as my cheerleader, my sage advisor, and my confidant at just the right times.

Lisa Polce

I dedicate this book to my son, Hunter John Polce, and to my parents. They are an inspiration to me. I am fortunate to have them in my life and they are, and always will be, the light of my life.

Contents

Acknowledgments

From Jim Smith

My deepest respect and thanks goes to my coauthor, Lisa Polce. She has a refreshing sense of integrity in everything she does. Writing this book with her has been an inspiration and has reinvigorated me as a Web design business owner to apply some of her great insights to my own business. As you read this book, I hope you find Lisa's sincerity and experience to be helpful as you start your new venture or improve upon the one you've already begun.

From Lisa Polce

When I was asked to cowrite this book, I was humbled and honored. The success of this book certainly will be due to the help and advice of my coauthor, Jim Smith. He never batted an eye in response to my endless questions about how to tackle each chapter. I am grateful for his constant support, friendship, and enthusiasm on this journey. It is not an easy road to get a book published.

Jim is a friend, colleague, and business confidant. We have worked on many projects together and have built a lasting friendship. I wouldn't be writing this book if Jim hadn't so graciously invited me to explore this opportunity. I'm honored and flattered that he thought enough of my work and skills as a graphic designer to join him as coauthor of this book.

Jim made each step seem easy to understand, and we worked together seamlessly. We make good book partners. What makes us work so great together is that we are good at what we do and we respect each other's talents. We sincerely want the other to succeed. I can't beat that when it comes to colleagues.

And, as always, I am grateful for the love, support, and understanding from my son, Hunter. May he enjoy the benefits of good, old-fashioned hard work. I spent many hours on my computer and laptop writing this book. I appreciate his patience. And to my mom and dad for teaching me that with hard work and steadfast determination, you can reach your goals. I try to be the best I can be every day, even when nobody is looking.

Introduction

When Jim Smith approached me to coauthor this book about how to set up and operate a home-based graphic design business, my first thought was: "Really? Me? What could I have to share with others about running a business?" I was humbled and honored that he asked me to contribute to this book. With the economy the way it is and many people out of work, more and more individuals are starting their own businesses. I don't think I just woke up one day and said, "I want to own my business." The opportunity presented itself to me while I was on unemployment and wanting to do something about it. I wish I'd had a book like this when I was trying to support myself on just the income generated by my business.

Until your new business moves beyond its growing pains and you are generating enough money to support yourself, which could take up to five years, I would recommend a nice cushion in the bank to get you through the slow periods, if possible. Or prepare for the peaks and valleys by having additional income from other sources. Owning your own business has its rewards, and it feels wonderful to be your own boss, but great feelings aside, you still need to pay your bills. The opportunities are out there. Reach for the stars and set goals for yourself. You *can* be successful, and I wish you all the luck and success one can achieve, but it won't be easy.

Just be practical about owning your business, and make sure you are making the right decisions for your situation. My contribution to this book comes from my own experience, and where noted, I have brought in professionals to offer their advice for owning a business. My experiences as a self-employed designer are just that—*my* opinions, *my* experiences, and *my* trial-and-error lessons.

Certainly you can develop your own style and methods for your business. I don't think there is a right or wrong way when it comes to personal style. Practical business methods aside, I would encourage you to be honest and trustworthy, and to treat your clients with respect and dignity. Customer service is an essential part of being successful. No matter what you do, always treat people the way you want to be treated. Customer service and simple communication with your clients keeps you ahead of the game. All you have to do is remember the last time you didn't have good customer service and how it made you feel. Don't let that feeling be from one of your clients.

Even if you eventually choose to dissolve your graphic design business to pursue other opportunities, I doubt that you will ever regret the decision to become a business owner. The process is a great learning experience, not just on the business end, but also in learning how to deal with people and handling all kinds of situations. In the long run, you certainly should be proud of yourself for trying. It definitely has been a humbling experience for me, and I am very proud that it has been part of my career path. There are good days and bad days, but that comes with the territory.

I hope this book will give you the confidence to take a leap of faith and start your business. Don't give up. Talk to and learn from your colleagues and people you meet along the way, and don't be afraid to adjust your business routine. Every day is a learning experience. As you gain experience as a business owner, what you did in the beginning might be totally different from what you do now.

It's a wonderful world out there, with endless opportunities. Situations will arise that force you to make some tough decisions, but those decisions will help your business grow into something you can be proud of. As Sir Thomas Buxton once said, "With ordinary talent and extraordinary perseverance, all things are attainable." I hope this book will help you on your journey and give you the confidence you need to attain your own successful home-based graphic design business. Then we both will have succeeded!

01 So You Want to Start a Home-based Graphic Design Business?

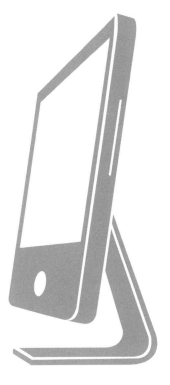

Why do you want to own your own business? There could be many reasons why you want to take a leap of faith and become a business owner. After I lost my job, I freelanced for several months. With some luck and good timing, I worked as an independent contractor for a local trade show and exhibit company. With those steady projects, as well as projects that I developed on my own, I got a pretty good idea of what it was like to be self-employed. If you are in between jobs, create some projects on your own to see if this is a good fit. Freelancing is a good way to get your feet wet. If you are sure you want to own your own business, I would suggest talking to a lawyer to see what direction you should go in. With the projects that were being generated from that trade show company, I stayed pretty busy and decided to become an official business owner.

Speaking of "why" you want to own your own business—and, really, the "why" of any important decision—the "why" should be pretty important to you. Even though my "why" and your "why" are most likely totally different, your "why" should involve some strong passion and depth. Your business should be so important to you that you are humbled by your own reasons for starting it. This "why" will be a constant reminder of why you decided to branch out on your own. Write it down, memorize it, and when things seem impossible and you feel like giving up, reread your "why."

My "why" is that I love what I do, and because of that passion, I have control of my decisions, my future, and my happiness. I care enough about what I do to want my clients to come back again and again. I want them to refer me to their friends. There are few feelings in business better than getting clients through word-of-mouth advertising. But most importantly, I am passionate about my business because I want to be able to provide for myself and my son, for now as well as for both of our futures.

My Advice

If you are considering self-employment, my first advice would be to ask yourself: Is this my passion? Do I love what I do? In reference to this book, do you love graphic design? I don't think most people just wake up one day and decide to start their own graphic design business. You need to have been in the field for a while and to have grasped the basic, if not intermediate, skills to keep up with the growth and changes within the industry. Do your homework. Learn the applications and skills first. I started my own business when I was laid off from a full-time position where I was getting a salary with benefits. I was devastated at the time, but I knew I wanted to stay in the graphic design field. To stay fresh with my skills, I started freelancing almost right away.

Now I have been in the industry over twenty years. Are there designers better than I am? Yes. Are there worse designers? Yes. I am constantly learning something in my arena, whether it's related to the business or the creative aspects. As a graphic designer, your skills are constantly growing.

It is not easy. Let me repeat: *Being self-employed is not easy*, nor is it guaranteed to be an immediate success. Success is not instantaneous; it comes with time. But if you persevere, you will have great results and be proud of them. It's a leap of faith. You are traveling on a path that you are not used to being on. Most likely, you were at a nine-to-five job, and when you left, your day was done. Well, this is not so much the case if you are self-employed. Sometimes it feels like your day never ends.

As of this writing, I have been self-employed for almost four years. There were times I cried. There were times I laughed. And, yes, I pondered the possibility that I might be able to make more money working for someone else. But, I can tell you this—I'm happy. I care about doing a great job every time. It's rewarding to turn a concept, notes scribbled on paper, into a design that will satisfy both the client and me when it is completed.

My clients and I work together really hard to get to the point at which we are satisfied. I will probably mention this a lot. My clients and I work as a team. I know graphic design, but they know their business better than I do. We come together to give that "great first impression" in their marketing materials. If their target audience doesn't read it, they won't keep it. Do you want the client's target audience to throw away your design? Of course not!

No two days are the same. I can be busy at my desk one day, and the next I'm out networking or meeting clients, buying supplies, or just observing what's going on around me. As a graphic designer, I find that my eye and mind are checking things out nonstop. Most call that people-watching. You can learn a lot by watching human behavior. What are the trends out there? Whom do you surround yourself with? How are others under the graphic design and advertising umbrella successful?

Being self-employed has been an awesome experience. Have I wanted to give up? Sometimes! Have I cried myself to sleep wondering if I'm going to make it? Sometimes. I think the hardest part is maintaining a steady stream of clients and sufficient cash flow to make it to the next step. Whatever challenges you face, stay strong and persevere. It is during the slow times that we learn the most. Successful business owners don't give up. Successful owners constantly sharpen their skills and hold their heads up high.

What Is Your Personality?

You are probably wondering what your personality has to do with running a business. Well, some people are not meant to be "their own boss." Some prefer being directed and told what to do. Others like to think and work independently. It doesn't make you a bad person if you don't want to be self-employed. I do think it takes a certain personality to want to be your own boss. It is not for the timid. If you are shy, take some public-speaking classes or look for a local Toastmasters club. You may feel uncomfortable talking in front of a group at first, but you need to work on being the star of the show. When you are networking with potential clients, you must always be "on."

Two of the most important traits you can carry are self-pride and self-worth. As in life, you must be able to get through those "low times" or "what am I doing being self-employed?" times. Sure, some days I have my doubts—even now. But I remind myself that my self-esteem will soon kick in so I can shake off this "down" feeling.

It comes down to this: Do you want to work for someone else or work for yourself? If you work for yourself, you have control of your day and your time. You must have the same stamina you would have if you reported to someone—manager, supervisor, or boss. But you will report to yourself. I am a tough boss on myself. If I have revisions in from a client, I make sure to get them done immediately.

Are you living up to your own standards? You'd better set those standards high. Set goals and work schedules, and just as importantly, schedule time for yourself to do things like going for an invigorating walk. Carve out some time to "turn your head off." It's healthy. On the other hand, there are times when I do not want to sit at my computer, but I push myself to do so.

Do You Have the Right Personality for Self-Employment?

Can you work independently?

_____

Are you organized?

_____

Do you pay attention to detail?

_____

Do you prioritize your daily tasks?

_____

Can you handle multitasking?

_____

Can you wear many hats?

_____

Can you schedule design projects according to deadlines?

_____

Can you work hard without someone looking over your shoulder?

_____

Can you work with the distractions in your home?

_____

Do you have what it takes to talk to people, network, and sell yourself and your business?

_____

Are you prepared for meetings?

_____

Are you passionate about what you do?

_____

What is your customer service level?

_____

These are just some questions to ask yourself when determining whether or not you have the right personality to be your own boss. I constantly work on this. I am humble enough to know that I can always do better.

One thing that does motivate me, and I frequently remind myself of this, is that if I don't work, I don't get paid. The sooner I get that proof out to a client, the closer I am to getting another invoice paid. I would love to say I get paid for all the meetings I attend. There is a lot of unbillable time to even get a client signed and ready to work on the project. It could be as long as a few weeks from the time I have my initial meeting to the time I accept the quote, receive a signed contract and deposit, and then actually start my designs.

Now let's talk a little about the personality questions in the above worksheet.

Can You Work Independently?

Some people need a lot of direction, supervision, and assistance to get through the tasks and responsibilities of their workday. When you are your own boss, you are the team, supervisor, sales staff, bookkeeper, cleaning person, buyer, and many more all wrapped up in your body and mind as the owner. You will have to be able to work independently with the knowledge of how much time you need to set aside for each task.

Are You Organized?

Well, this can go in a lot of different directions. Maybe your definition of organized is totally different from mine. Did you ever walk into an office where everything is strewn everywhere? You just don't know how they can work like that. If you're disorganized yourself, that's not a good image to project to clients.

When you work from home, you must stay organized in every aspect of your workday: when you wake up, how you start your day, what's on the agenda, what you need to accomplish for the day, and making sure your physical surroundings are organized. Keep in mind that I am talking about not just your business day, but also keeping your home life organized. Being organized takes you one step closer to wrapping up a project and sending the invoice. One thing I will add here: If you have space in your home office where you can meet with clients, that area needs to look professional and clean. Not having a clean, orderly area can kill a prospect's decision to hire you. As I write this book, I do not have a dedicated space in my home to meet clients. Instead, I meet them at their offices or somewhere convenient for the both of us, such as a coffee shop.

Do You Pay Attention to Detail?

This can be a big asset to your business. An important part of being organized is paying attention to detail. Think of how you would like to be treated when you are making a major decision about your money and where to spend it. Paying attention to details—right down to how you represent yourself, your work, your proofs, and your ability to follow through—can make or break you. The list goes on. You don't want to come across as a scatterbrain.

Do You Prioritize Your Daily Tasks?

Do you ever have those days when you've worked and worked, but everything of any importance is still lingering? Part of staying organized is prioritizing your tasks. Otherwise, there is a tendency to work on either the easiest or most fun tasks first. Create a list of what you need to accomplish and then assign high, medium, and low priorities, or even number your list from most to least critical.

Can You Handle Multitasking?

This falls under paying attention to detail and being organized. If you can multitask, you are one step closer to being successful. You'll need to be able to juggle multiple projects in different stages of design, the phone ringing, answering e-mails—you get the picture. Multitasking—and doing it well, without sacrificing quality—is a true skill.

Can You Wear Many Hats?

When you are self-employed, you are a one-man show. Wearing many hats can get overwhelming. The number of hats can vary depending on what services you offer, but remember that you are running a business. Look at what it takes to run a successful company and how many people are needed to run it. Well, you are all those people rolled into one.

■ **Boss hat:** How is the business running? Are you meeting your goals? What can you do better? What are you doing right? You are the boss. Part of that is making the tough decisions. You will need to put on your boss hat when it is time to talk to a nice client who is late in paying. You will need the boss hat when the sales are in a slump and it is time to take on a low-paying client so you can survive for the better days ahead. The boss faces the stressful decisions so the business will flourish.

- **Sales hat:** You are the sales staff. How are you representing the business? Are you on time for appointments, following up with leads, or getting quotes out? How much new business is coming in, and how much repeat business are you getting? What meetings are scheduled? What kind of meetings are they: networking, client-oriented, follow-up, or answering any questions the clients may have?

- **Customer service hat:** Customer service, customer service, customer service. I can't say it enough. Treat all your clients as if only they matter. Treat clients with respect, and appreciate their time and business. You should be setting time aside to send thank-you notes—you know, the kind that goes in the mail and the client actually opens. People do not do enough thank-you correspondence anymore. I don't mean a text or e-mail, but an actual card. Make it a point to send one out. Use your logo and contact information, and thank clients for their time, business, or networking. Don't forget to sign the card. It will mean a lot. I know it makes me feel good when I get a card in the mail. It sounds so simple, but it's a way to stand out in your client's mind.

- **Bookkeeper hat:** Ah, this can be tedious for our creative minds: keeping track of your business finances. Are you going to do it yourself or hire someone? Running a home-based business involves preparing a budget, entering receipts, getting quotes and invoices out, keeping track of your billable time, and filing taxes (including sales and quarterly) on time. I probably didn't know all these elements starting out. I learned to pay attention to them.

- **Administrative hat:** This involves some bookkeeping items, responding to e-mails, budgeting your time and daily schedule, making phone calls, staying organized, and answering clients' questions.

You may find that you have other hats to wear. In any event, wearing multiple hats means that you must stay organized and pay attention to detail.

Can You Schedule Design Projects According to Deadlines?

Prioritize. What needs to get done now, at lunchtime, and later in the day? Are you meeting your project deadlines? We don't live in a perfect world. You will have mitigating circumstances that might cause you to miss a deadline. Be honest, maintain open communication, and let the client know. Your best policy is no surprises. I work best with a list. I write down what needs to be done and then decide what needs to be done first. Sometimes my day detracts from the plan. When some things take longer than expected, adjust accordingly. Write things down. It's good for recording billable time and to see how long design tasks are taking you.

Can You Work Hard without Someone Looking over Your Shoulder?

In other words, do you have enough discipline to work independently, as I mentioned above? You must take this seriously. It's like when you were in college, juggling your social and academic life. You knew what would happen if you didn't leave enough time to study for a test or to write a paper. Well, it's the same thing with your work-from-home ethic. Work hard, whether someone is looking or not. I'll mention it again: If you don't work, you don't get paid.

Can You Work with the Distractions in Your Home?

I'm going to continue with home distractions: getting up to eat; watching TV; tending to household issues, your children, your spouse, your home life, etc. The list goes on, but you get the gist. It's easy to stop to eat, and then the mail comes, the phone rings, and the laundry needs to be done. Adjust your schedule so you have time to juggle everything. It is a good idea to take a break from your computer and office surroundings. Just do it with discipline.

Do You Have What It Takes to Talk to People, Network, and Sell Yourself and Your Business?

Unfortunately, business doesn't come knocking on your door all the time. You have to generate your next client or sale. When you are self-employed, you must feel comfortable talking with people and being in front of people. This can mean one-on-one meetings or networking with a roomful of people you don't know, but you will need to be comfortable with the idea. Guess what? You get better every time you do it. Trust me. Remember, you are the sales staff, too.

This is what I meant by being observant. Your next client doesn't have to come from a meeting. If you train yourself to listen and pick up on what is going around you, your next client isn't too far away. Be professional, be honest, be polite, and smile even if it kills you. You will have to get out of your comfort zone. Every meeting is like a mini interview. This could be a potential client, or maybe the person knows someone who needs your services. Always be professional.

Are You Prepared for Meetings?

Whenever you have a meeting with a potential client or are networking, you need to be prepared. Do you have business cards? Are your samples or portfolio ready? Be prepared to take notes. Be on time. If something comes up that detains you, make sure you have a contact number to let the person know. Listen. I know that sounds obvious, but be patient, listen to the person talking, act interested, care about what the person is saying. Sometimes it's not all business.

Are You Passionate about What You Do?

Can you say "I love what I do"? Part of being a good salesperson is knowing what you are talking about. If you are passionate about what you do, it will come out naturally. People will recognize that in you. They want to do business with people who can handle themselves and speak well of what they do. Part of getting any business, whether it is a new client or repeat business, is building a good reputation. And getting business these days is harder than you think. You have to be better than your competition, and you have to offer something that your competition doesn't. Along with those obstacles, you have to expose your business. If you aren't passionate about what you do, it will show in your meetings. If you are serious about starting a home-based graphic design business, you have to love what you do.

What Is Your Customer Service Level?

Are you ready to adopt the "customer is always right" principle? Think about the last time you were waited on or asked for a salesperson's advice. How did you feel when you had great customer service? How did you feel when the customer service wasn't very good? Whether in person or on the phone, smile. Part of being a business owner is having great customer service skills. Do you get back to clients in a timely manner in all areas: phone, e-mails, contracts, meeting deadlines, or delivering projects? Remember to treat people how you want to be treated—in business and in life. Customer service starts with the handshake and continues all the way through to the finished project, and beyond. Customer service is part of paying attention to detail.

Can You Handle Being on Your Own?

Are you ready to be self-employed? Are you scared to start your own business? Well, you should be. You are taking a huge emotional, physical, and financial risk. Are you ready for that "leap of faith" into the unknown? It's scary out there in the "real world."

Running your own business takes a lot of hard work. I am not trying to sound cliché, but it's certainly not easy. Yes, it is rewarding, but every day is a challenge. In a "corporate position," your work comes to you. When you own your own graphic design business, you have to get projects by constantly selling and pushing yourself. No one is there to tell you what to do because you are your own boss.

Do you have the discipline to work and play? Are you willing to work late at night or through the weekend to meet a deadline? Being self-employed is not for the lazy. Be honest with yourself. If you are not ready for the long hours and hard work, a home-based business may not be for you.

You may feel intimidated by the number of home-based graphic designers out there. Put that fear aside—or, better yet, meet it head on. Sure, it's scary. There isn't that steady paycheck anymore. Part of starting your own business is being courageous and having faith that you can make it. Success doesn't come overnight. You constantly have to expose your business. You have no one else to rely on but yourself.

As you get started with your business, pool your resources with outside talents so you can present yourself as being part of a team. Those outside talents can include a professional photographer, Web designer, copywriter, or quality printer. These professionals can become your partners and your team. If you are confident about working independently and are disciplined with a strong work ethic, you will do just fine.

There are definitely benefits to self-employment. You are your own boss. You have your own schedule. You can work whenever you want. You can create a great work environment. Mine just happens to be my house. I love what I do, and being creative seems to be where my head likes to go. However, it is very challenging, and it comes with its ups and downs.

I wish I could wave a magic wand and say that being self-employed will bring you instant success. If you have taken the soul-searching step and answered that question, "Am I ready to own my own business?" with a resounding yes, then you are one step closer to becoming successful.

What Skills Do You Need to Be Successful?

What skills do you need to be successful? Well, that's a loaded question. If you try and don't give up, then you are probably going to be successful. Some skills are obvious, such as knowing the software applications and staying on top of design trends—which, as you probably already know, are constantly changing.

You need to be computer-savvy. Technology is never at a standstill. As soon as you master a level of the Adobe Creative Suite, a new version comes out with all kinds of cool tricks to learn. There are some great websites out there for tricks and tips of the creative world. Adobe has online chats and forums where you can post questions about its programs. This really helps you keep your skills current. You can see the different answers, and if you follow the posts, you can learn something. Adobe products come with interactive help right in each individual application. The website Lynda.com offers webinars and videos on current trends and the latest applications for all of the creative industry. The site is very easy to use, and subscriptions are relatively inexpensive.

There are also intangible skills. One trait that has to be there no matter what is honesty. Be honest with your work ethic, honest with yourself, and honest about your hours and pricing. Remember, you have to live with yourself. You have to look that client in the eye.

If you are a one-person show, you have to balance your priorities. Your pricing needs to be fair. Projects differ depending on what's involved, so it can be hard to establish a set fee for a brochure, but be fair with your pricing. The price you offer one person should be comparable to what you offer the next.

Designing is what makes you money, but organization, attention to detail, bookkeeping, writing quotes and contracts, following up with clients and potential clients, and researching design projects all deserve 120 percent of your attention. Notice how I didn't say 100 percent; I said 120 percent. You have to push yourself. Just remember, your skills are constantly changing, and you are redefining and refining those skills to keep them sharp. How I was as a businessperson when I first started has changed as I've gained more experience in the self-employment world.

I like meeting my clients and prospects face-to-face when possible. Sure, you can have clients outside your local area and never meet them, but you lose that personal touch. I have clients that live all over the country and I still maintain a successful business relationship with them. I do think there is an extra touch to meeting face-to-face, ideally on multiple occasions, to help the relationship grow.

Relationships are a two-way street. This isn't just about when the project is in progress, but also after it is over. Stay in touch with your clients, whether it's a quick note to say hello or checking in to see if they need anything. It seems simple, but it works. Your clients are people, too. Treat them as people, not just as clients. Most people do business with people they like and know. People care when you care.

This is one of the many times when being comfortable with yourself and representing yourself well come into play. Hold your head up high, and have a great handshake and smile. Leave any shyness at the door. It should be easy if you love what you do. It is easy to talk about what you enjoy doing, and it is easy to talk about something you feel confident about. Self-confidence is the key here.

Then there are the sales skills. You are your own salesperson. Are you comfortable talking about your business, your services, and what sets you apart from your competition? If you are shy, then work on speaking in front of people, because being self-employed is not for the shy. Can you work on those skills and overcome shyness? Absolutely! But you will have to come out of your shell and be ready to shine in front of individuals and groups. I talk about networking in chapter 9.

Creative skills are constantly growing and changing. Depending on your starting capital, maybe you have access to experts in the industry that you can bring into the project. Think of them as your staff, whether they are there for a single project or multiple contracts.

The last great skill you must have is customer service. People like to be treated right. Graphic designers (at least *this* graphic designer) treat clients as a team. Without the client, a design project will not be a success, nor will it be something you want to brag about later.

Customer service does not end when you get clients. It's a continuous process. Be thankful they hired your company. It's harder to get new clients than to keep existing ones. So send thank-you cards and sign off on e-mails to clients by thanking them for their business. These little details can make a huge difference.

Keep in mind that the word "skill" is thrown around a lot. As a one-person show, you will wear many hats, and sometimes more than one at a time. I would recommend that you *not* be a jack-of-all-trades but master of none. Really hone in on what sets you apart from your competition. Don't forget about the art of communication. Be professional, dress the part, and communicate professionally with your clients.

How Will You Know If You Have What It Takes?

How do you know if you have what it takes to be self-employed as a graphic designer? I've answered a lot of that in the previous paragraphs. I feel confident that I have what it takes. How do I know that? Well, I'm still in business, right? Believe me, it takes guts, a leap of faith, and strong determination to make it work.

A relatively easy way to test the waters before you form an LLC (limited liability company), name your business, pay business entity and sales taxes, etc., is to freelance for a while. "Freelance" sounds like being self-employed. A lot of people get the two mixed up. To me, being self-employed means having a named business. Anyone can say, "I freelance." I do not freelance; I own and run a business. Freelancing is something you do on the side. You have to be careful here: Some companies don't like you freelancing or doing your trade outside of the company.

If your company is amenable to freelancing, get some small jobs started. Handle them professionally and accurately. Once you have a few freelance projects under your belt, it can be a make-or-break time for you as a potential business owner. Just be honest with yourself.

Questions to Ask Yourself after Your First Project

- How did I prepare myself to meet the client?

- Was I accurate with the pricing of the design project?

- Did I meet the deadlines?

- Did I have accurate knowledge of the project?

- Did I get paid in a timely manner?

- How was my customer service?

- Will this client come back for other design projects?

- How did I like the process?

- Was I disciplined to get the project done right, on time and within budget?

How to Handle Friendly Competition

Do not be afraid of friendly competition. The places you visit or network as a self-employed designer will expose you to competition. I used to think, "Oh, great, another graphic designer." But after a while I started thinking about how I could set myself apart from the competition.

When you are around competitors, please remember to be professional. Don't talk behind their backs. Don't discredit them. Remember, would you want to have that done to you? I even meet other graphic designers for coffee and share information and stories. Every time, I have learned something about myself and things I can do better. I have had graphic designers call me for advice or to look over their designs. We have shared advice about how to handle certain situations.

It's healthy to meet others in your field. You don't need to give away any of your secrets or disclose your client list to them, but it is nice to learn that there are other talented graphic designers experiencing the same ups and downs that you're facing.

How to Strengthen Any Weaknesses

How can you work on problem areas to make yourself better? Every day that you are self-employed is a learning experience. Every day that you have survived being your own boss is an accomplishment. Just as in life, do you say "I am the best I can be?" Do you ask yourself, "Can I be better at what I do?" Never get complacent, because while you are busy maintaining the status quo, your competition is becoming better than you are. I don't think I am an expert. Am I good—or even great—at what I do? Yes. Am I at the top, never needing to learn something new? No.

You can sharpen your strengths even when you are not thinking about it. I would stay away from the word "weak" to define areas that need work. Instead, you should ask yourself, "What can I improve upon?" Make your strengths even stronger and improve on the areas that need sharpening. Do you enter the self-employment world knowing everything there is to know about running a successful graphic design business? Of course not. What I knew when I first started and what I know now are leaps and bounds apart. And I am still growing. I still experience growing pains, trying to figure out what works and what doesn't. I am constantly adjusting to the ups and downs of running my own business.

As I mentioned earlier, part of running your own business is keeping on top of your skills and current technology. Read articles, talk to colleagues, and take webinars and online courses that interest you. Be gentle with yourself. Take one step at a time as far as improvements. Don't ever think you can't learn something, because you can. Don't ever think you are too old to take a class, because you are not. I am flattered when colleagues ask me their opinion, so don't be afraid to ask questions. Talk to friends and people you respect in the business. Talk to other business owners outside the design industry.

The simple act of identifying an area to improve upon and seeking information is a strength. Nobody is perfect, but we all try to be perfect in a not-so-perfect world. Take it one step at a time. Know that anyone who has started his or her own business was not perfect right out of the gate. Learning how you can improve in areas that are not as strong as you would like them to be is good. Practice. Ask questions. Talk to industry leaders. Read information about design trends. Pick some areas that you want to improve on and, when you feel that you have succeeded, move on to another area. This doesn't pertain to just design skills, but all aspects of running your own business.

Envisioning the Business

When you start to plan your home-based graphic design business, it is important that you have a clear vision of the components of the business. Imagine you have a crystal ball and can get a glimpse of how your business is going to look. As with any usage of a magical crystal ball, if you can peer into the future now, you might just be able to direct the future your way. Here are some considerations for envisioning your business:

1. How big you visualize your business becoming
2. The components that will make up your business
3. The long-term future you see for your business

Let's look at each of these.

How Big You Visualize Your Business Becoming

A home-based business is usually thought of as a one-person business. But that is not necessarily the case. Do you have a spouse you plan to bring into your business? Do you envision a staff of illustrators creating marketing designs for your business? Do you want to add staff and grow as the demands of the business puts that pressure on you?

You are likely starting your home-based graphic design business because you enjoy graphic design. It is very likely that, as a creative graphic designer, you don't really care for the day-to-day grind of running a business. And you may not get pleasure out of the hiring and firing responsibilities of a large graphic design firm.

That is why it is important for you to develop a vision of your business now, rather than letting the day-to-day direction of your business dictate how it develops. If you know up front that you are not fond of managing a group of people, but your vision is to grow your home-based business into a large graphic design studio with several people, you can plan ahead to hire the right employee or partner who enjoys managing staffing issues.

The Components That Will Make Up Your Business

Part of planning your business comes from an assessment of the types of graphic design services you will be offering. Are you going to offer animations? Will your focus be on corporate branding? Package design? Illustrations?

Much of what you offer will depend on your skill set, but another consideration will be the marketability of your skills. Let's look at some of your options.

Illustration

An illustrator can cover a lot of areas. For the sake of coming up with ideas for your graphic design business, think of an illustrator as someone who creates sketches or drawings to integrate a visual image (illustration) with written text. A good example of an illustrator is an artist who creates images for children's books.

Technical Drawing

Whether it's a sketch of a refrigerator in a newspaper ad or a how-to diagram in a product manual, technical drawings are a necessary form of graphic design for manufacturers and advertising agents.

Web Design

Many Web designers are strong in technology but not as strong in graphics. That lack of graphic talent can be covered up with the use of templates. However, when customers want a unique look for their websites, many graphic designers have discovered a nice symbiotic relationship between the technical skills of a Web developer and the artistic abilities of a graphic designer.

Advertising and Marketing

Advertising agencies generally find it convenient to have one or more graphic designers available to create visually appealing advertisements for their clients. It is important for any graphic designer working on marketing designs not to fall in love with the design. The purpose of the design is not necessarily to impress the viewer; it is to motivate the viewer to buy a product or service. Beginner graphic designers who try to impress with an overly ornate design have their work classified as "eye candy"—sugary-sweet to the eye with no real substance.

Animation

When a business owner needs an animated (moving) clip to tell a story or to make a point, it is necessary to have an animator create the design. For example, if someone comes to you wanting to depict its solar panel that tracks the sun across the sky, that client is likely looking for an animator who can create a series of screens showing how the solar panel follows the sun.

Typography

This is the business of creating and manipulating fonts. Before it became mostly automated, typesetting was a major component of typography. If you have seen a stop sign and noticed that the font (all uppercase), the background color, and even the shape are all designed intentionally to maximize its utility, you might be skilled at typography. Most of us just accept signage, font layout, and other typography elements without realizing the reasoning behind each of those decisions.

Industrial Design

This incorporates art and science to improve a product's usability and marketability. Although the industrial designer's primary function is to develop manufactured products, he may also be called upon to prepare illustrations and sketches, and frequently even produce simulated models of industrial products. Designs such as the wide variety of rotary phones dating from the 1930s to their replacement with touch-tone phones are good examples of industrial design at its finest. With a range of modifications, rotary phones and their handsets became a symbol of the merging of design and art.

Informational Design

With the increase in data provided by the computer age, it is important for that information to be not only available, but also easy to understand. Informational designers provide layouts and design for data. This includes graphs and any other creative methods of illustrating the avalanche of data we face.

Cartoons

This field is vital for businesses and organizations trying to impart information in a light and palatable manner. Cartoonists can also be involved in animation or may work with animators to provide motion cartoons. Although some cartoonists provide their work solely for entertainment, many companies engage cartoonists to capture certain thoughts in a fun and lively manner.

Logo Design

A logo designer can be vital to an organization trying to impart the perfect image for its business. Numerous studies have indicated that a corporate logo is the most important aspect of branding a business. Coca-Cola's ribbonlike logo can be recognized in many countries thanks to its distinctive design. If someone questions the power of a logo, chop up some familiar logos and ask that person if he or she recognizes the company from the snippet of the logo. It is surprising how small a portion of a logo can still carry company recognition. Logo designers for large companies spend a lot of time creating and tweaking a logo's design to make sure it is just right.

Corporate Branding

This is the ability to match all components of a company, such as the logo, brochures, business cards, website, the appearance of the building, and more. When feasible, brandable components of a company should be designed to enhance the corporate image. Without a graphic design professional maintaining a company's brand, the logo and all of the markings that make up the brand get diluted.

Videography

A videographer does more than just capture moving images on a digital medium. A videographer typically designs the video, too.

Layout

Layout artists match text and images in an effective manner. They used to start out as paste-up artists, but with the tools available now, entry-level paste-up artists are no longer necessary. A layout artist's handiwork is most easily seen in the design of a magazine cover. It is important for text and images to be laid out to capture the attention of readers, so layout artists are frequently brought in to provide the maximum impact.

Package Design

Whereas many graphic designers deal with designs on flat surfaces, package designers work in a 3-D world. Packaged products need to be designed, as the package serves as the visual stimulus that frequently determines whether or not a shopper purchases a given product. If you look at the soda aisle, you will see some very creative and artistic bottles and packaging. It is important in product package design to stand out among all the competing products on the store shelf.

What Services Will You Offer?

Here's a roundup of the services your home-based graphic design business might include:

- ❑ Illustration
- ❑ Technical drawing
- ❑ Web design
- ❑ Advertising and marketing
- ❑ Animation
- ❑ Typography
- ❑ Industrial design
- ❑ Informational design
- ❑ Cartoons
- ❑ Logo design
- ❑ Corporate branding
- ❑ Videography
- ❑ Layout
- ❑ Package design

The Long-Term Future You See for Your Business

One part of envisioning your business that might not occur to you is looking beyond the normal business vision to the day you close your doors. What will that day look like? Now, don't start telling yourself that you never will close your business or shrug off that idea as unimportant. Take a deep look into that crystal ball and see where you want to take your business. Starting a home-based business isn't nearly as scary if you plan it out rather than just hope for the best!

Can you visualize the day you close your doors? Is it when you are wildly success-ful and retiring? Did you just sell the business to a young, ambitious person eager to please your long list of customers? Or did you have a family member who has learned the business over time and is ready to start walking in your footsteps? It will be much easier for you to chart a course to the day you close your doors if you can envision it before you even get started.

As you will see in chapter 4 ("Writing a Business Plan"), when you have a clear road map that spells out how to get to your mileposts, with a clear vision of how your business will end, you will have a much greater chance of success than if you allow the business to dictate how it will run itself.

The wonderful thing about a home-based graphic design business is that if you want to retire gradually while still working in your business, you can do that. When you are first starting your business, you will likely need to take every bit of work you can find. But once you are successful and looking at retirement, you can start cherry-picking the customers you want to work with on a part-time basis while telling oth-ers that you are limiting your workload. For some of you, that would be a wonderful reflection to have peering back from the crystal ball.

It is your business, and you get to choose how it should develop and how it should end. Just plan for it and follow your vision.

The "What If" Scenario

The other advantage to creating such a complete vision for your business is that you might discover a need for something else—a plan for the unlikely event that you get injured or face some other circumstance that renders you unable to deliver your commitments in a timely fashion. If that happens, do you have someone who can temporarily take over for you? Does someone have access to any files or designs that your clients may need?

Such a plan might seem like an unnecessary exercise, but your major clients are going to wonder what will happen to their originals or their work should you get hit by a bus while crossing the street. You should have an answer for that question should it arise. When it does (and someday it will!), it will be your largest potential cli-ent so far. They likely will not feel comfortable asking outright but will try to hem and haw their way through it. You can set their minds at ease if you jump in and lighten the mood by saying, "So what you are asking is what will happen to your project if I get squished by a bus, right?" Have a good answer and they will feel reassured that you have considered their needs throughout the project. And, of course, you should think through that same question if you plan to have an associate or family member take over the business someday. You do not necessarily know when that day may arrive, so give everyone the peace of mind knowing that you have a complete vision of your business.

03 | What Do You Need in Your Home Office?

Home office—does that sound cozy? One advantage of having a home business is that you can keep the overhead down and save money. Still, starting your own business can be scary all by itself. I think lines can get blurred when you work at home. People don't take you seriously. When you run into acquaintances, they might say, "Did you find a job yet?" I say, "I do have a job. I run my own business." Sometimes working from home commands less respect. That is one of those "I have to shake this off" times.

I would suggest having a dedicated area for your office. If you have a household that includes other people, make sure they are aware of your "office space." If you are lucky enough to have an entire room that can be your office, you are one step ahead of the game. But if you are like me, my office space is a corner of my kitchen. Try really hard to keep it uncluttered and organized. You need space to think, create, design, and run a business. If you tend to be messy, a home office may not be for you. I try to keep my area clean and organized, but that just happens to be part of my personality. I would love to have an "office space" outside my home, but I haven't graduated to that yet. And having a home office definitely saves me money, so I know I am being sensible about it. When you are ready to make the move, you can certainly move to an office space.

When you are starting out, you are a one-person show, which means that you are everything to the business: the administrative assistant, bookkeeper, salesperson, phone answerer, e-mail manager, follower of hot leads, maker of appointments, schedule coordinator, and most importantly, lest you forget, the graphic designer. Designing brings the money in for your business. So, like I said, stay organized. It is critical to your home office success. Sometimes you have to get creative with the space available and adapt it to suit your needs.

In a perfect world and with my expensive taste, I would love everything new, but I don't live in a perfect world. I learned that I could get by with what I had at first. Then, when the money started coming in, I could do a little at a time and buy things I wanted, not just things I needed. I'm sure you have heard of this before, the concept of need versus want.

I would recommend that you be very particular with your computer and printer. You need to have up-to-date equipment. This can be a sore subject because technology is changing all the time, as are the applications that we use to make a living. Be sensible about it. I believe that your computer and applications should be new. Once you purchase the applications you need to design, the upgrades for the applications are cost-effective. But everything doesn't have to be new. You can get by with used equipment, but be realistic about it. Some things are critical to a home office; other items can wait for another time or when there is more steady income.

What You Need in Your Home Office

LOCATION
- ❏ Dedicated area
- ❏ Uncluttered area (organization skills)
- ❏ Area to meet clients

FURNITURE
- ❏ Desk
- ❏ Comfortable chair
- ❏ Drafting table (or area where you can put working proofs together)
- ❏ File cabinet

EQUIPMENT AND TOOLS
- ❏ Computer
- ❏ Software applications
- ❏ Printer (including all-in-one printer, scanner, fax, copier)
- ❏ Internet and e-mail browser
- ❏ Phone
- ❏ Supplies (ink, various printer paper sizes, pencils, paper clips, etc.)
- ❏ Good lighting
- ❏ Music

The items in the checklist are just some of what could make up your office. You can start slow with the above equipment. If you have the money, by all means, get everything you need in the beginning. But it's not critical to your success. Let's look at each of those items individually.

Location

Dedicated Area

Your dedicated office area needs to be a space where, when you enter, you feel you are at work. It should be a place in your home where you can tune things out and concentrate on the task at hand. Sometimes you don't have the space to dedicate an entire room to the office, but make sure it feels like your work area—not a family room, not a living room, but an area where you can be productive despite the distractions. If you need to have a Do Not Disturb sign or office hours, then do that. As I mentioned before, there is sometimes a fine line between having a home business and having a home life.

Maybe I'm repeating myself here, but I want to emphasize again the importance of being disciplined. To run a successful home business, you must have self-discipline, ambition, and a strong work ethic. Sorry to be blunt, but if you know you are the lazy type, then perhaps a home business isn't for you. Make time to work. Don't look at the mail, don't read the newspaper, don't sleep late, and don't watch those morning shows. Get to work! Being your own boss is great, but be hard on yourself when it comes to working hard. I've said it before, and I'll say it again: If you don't work, you don't get paid. And, of course, if you don't get paid, you can't pay your bills. When you own your own business, you can make your own hours, so to speak; just realize that if you miss deadlines, the first person you disappoint will be yourself. Stay focused and disciplined regarding deadlines and meeting clients' expectations.

Remember, too, that it's important to take a break. Step away from the desk. Close your eyes, exercise, make a cup of tea, go for a walk, or spend some time with your dog (if you have one). It's important to break up your routine a little bit. Sometimes I feel like I have writer's block—or, for us designers, designer's block. There needs to be a good balance between working hard and stepping away for a bit. As your own boss, you make your own hours. Balance your schedule carefully.

Ideally, your work area should be relatively quiet and have some level of privacy. When I say privacy, it sounds like I mean being secretive. What I mean by privacy is a quiet area, an area in which you can talk without worrying who is overhearing you. Graphic design isn't Secret Service work, but you are running a business. Many clients appreciate it when you treat their upcoming corporate events confidentially.

When you were at your nine-to-five job before becoming self-employed, you probably noticed that your work area had a flow to it. Well, it's the same here in your home office. Part of creating a dedicated area is making sure you have a nice flow to your work. It sounds crazy, but some people work better left to right; others work better right to left. Is it more comfortable to answer the phone with your left or right hand? Where you put your equipment is vital. Just like having a system in place for the administrative part of your business, the work flow of your area is important. Call it the Zen of your office or even the feng shui of your work area. Just set it up to suit your work flow so that your day has some type of personal rhythm. You'll see what I mean once you start working. If it feels awkward, change it around. You are the boss now!

Uncluttered Area

Don't be a slob. Okay, easier said than done. I am a neat person. I like things in their place. Part of running your own business is staying organized. If your office is in a part of the home that clients will have access to, you have to look professional and stay neat. Make yourself do it. When you don't have a lot of space, you need to get creative with how you use the space, storage, and equipment that will make up the office. If your home office is messy, it can lead to frustration. Create a professional space that meets your basic needs and style. The more you feel you are at home, the more you run the risk of not focusing on the task at hand. There will be more chances of getting distracted.

Area to Meet Clients

I haven't graduated to office space outside of my home. Therefore, I prefer to meet clients at an area coffee shop, quaint restaurant, or their office. Any time you meet a client, treat it like a professional meeting. Project a professional image and appearance.

Another good option for client meetings is the use of technology, such as a video or conference call. For the most part, meeting face-to-face is great, but for occasional meetings, video conferencing will work. I would use some caution here. For video conferencing to be productive, your client should be tech-savvy, and there could be an expense associated with this type of communication as far as proper equipment.

You should be careful when meeting potential clients. Unfortunately, we have to keep our guard up and use common sense, especially if it's a potential client you don't know who contacted you through your website.

Furniture

Desk

The desk I started with was from my college days. I have improved upon that since, but I didn't run out and buy a new one. A desk should have enough space for the computer, an area for your most current projects, a notepad, etc. Just the desk alone is crucial to your work flow and not feeling cramped. These are just suggestions, of course. Everyone has their own desk setup that makes them comfortable.

Comfortable Chair

You don't have to buy a new chair, but make sure it's comfortable for being at the computer and sitting at your desk for long periods of time. You will need good support and proper height. As I write this book, I need a new chair. There are all kinds of office chairs out there—leather, cloth, faux leather, tweed, executive back, etc. It's like a bed: Sit in one, try it out. Some are more comfortable than others. Does it swivel? Does it have wheels? This may sound silly, but go shopping and actually sit and squirm around in some chairs before buying one. You are the one that will be sitting in it for hours at a time.

Drafting Table

We are designers. We are constantly putting files together that need assembling. Brochures, double-sided business cards, packaging, really anything with more than one page, and anything bigger than 8.5 x 11. You can certainly print reduced files, but I like to have a true-size version so you can really see what things will look like. You want to see what it looks like on paper, where things fold, whether the folds are right. Adequate space for that is important. An X-Acto knife and a good ruler are a must. Make sure your X-Acto knife is sharp. Dull blades can rip your edges. Remember, you are eventually showing the client a proof. You want it to look as good as possible. Designs can look great on the screen, but you have to print them to see what they really look like on paper. That sounds simple, but some people don't do it.

It is great to be able to have both a drafting table and a desk, but if you can only have a desk when you start out, make sure that you use material to protect the surface.

File Cabinet

I am a neat person, so I tend to be really organized. Especially if you have several projects at once, all in different stages of design, you need to have a filing system. Do what works for you, but, and I can't stress this enough, stay organized. You always want to be prepared when someone calls or if you need to reference a project. There is no right or wrong way, as long as it makes sense to you.

A filing system has to be part of a formal procedure in your routine. I use folders within hanging folders. I usually keep "old" files in the back and more current files in the front. You can keep them alphabetically, by month, by name of client—whatever system makes sense to you and makes it easy to find what you are looking for. I keep the most current projects in a wire frame that has progressive levels. Prevalent projects sometimes even stay on my desk. Older projects get filed away in the file cabinet.

This all goes back to multitasking. I try to keep projects revolving, giving them the priority they need. This means not only client files, but also files that involve tracking my business, such as accurate bookkeeping, paying invoices, and logging time and even mileage. Establishing these as formal procedures keeps you organized. Devote time to your filing system a little each day so that you don't feel overwhelmed. As your own boss, you must wear several hats at once.

Equipment and Tools

Computer

Well, this is always a heated debate, but let me start with this—you have to have an updated computer. Invest in a good one that offers the graphics, memory, and speed you need to work. Technology is constantly changing. Something that doesn't meet your basic requirements is just going to lead to frustration down the road. We graphic designers need great graphics and performance, really good monitors, and lots of memory for all our files. Do your homework and research what's best for what you are trying to accomplish and what your budget can handle.

Desktops vs. Laptops

Should you buy a desktop or laptop computer? There are so many choices out there with various advantages, features, and price points. Choosing a desktop versus a laptop depends on how you would use either one. Will you be away from your desk a lot?

Laptops are just as powerful as desktops. I have both. I like using my desktop as my home base. My laptop is much newer than my desktop, though, and it's great when I just want to get out of the house. My laptop is also awesome when I need to show clients something on the screen, go over a proof, or do revisions right on the spot.

You can easily run a home business on a laptop. One thing about a home office is that it's still your home. Having a laptop allows you to travel when it's nice out or you just want a change of scenery from your home office. You can get out of the house without feeling guilty and do yourself some good by working in a new environment. I even bought a wireless mouse for my laptop, as I found it hard to design with the little square touchpad that typically comes on a laptop.

It used to be that desktops were king, the ultimate piece of office equipment. Laptops have come a long way and are becoming the staple of an office. Laptops are sleek, classy, and equipped with a lot of power these days. They are getting thinner and lighter, but they still can perform like a desktop. Desktops still come with plenty of power and memory, and you can work with many programs open when you need to multitask. Laptops often have low battery life, which means if you are working without being plugged in, you need to charge your laptop every few hours.

There are certainly advantages and disadvantages to each. It will come down to what you prefer and expect from your computer. Research what you are looking for in a computer, and do what makes you comfortable. It is certainly a personal decision.

While I am on the subject of computers, I need to mention backing up your work. If you have ever been in a situation where you didn't back up your work and—*wham!*—something happened, you likely learned the value of backups the hard way. This can be something as simple as not saving your work that was open when you lost power or as complex as not backing up your files to an external hard drive on a regular basis. One of the most important things you can buy is an external hard drive. Get your archived work files off your computer and save them somewhere else. This helps with computer memory, keeps you organized, and gives you peace of mind. Another option that is becoming popular is backing up files online (SkyDrive, Carbonite, etc.). If you are considering an online backup, take advantage of the free trials to make sure it doesn't slow you down.

I am sure you have, at one time or another, lost a file because you failed to back it up or did not save often. Again, it is imperative to do this regularly. I've had clients call me a few years after I completed a project for them because they want to revise or update it. I sure am glad I backed up those files. They are easy to find, and I can retrieve them without spending hours searching.

Another tip about backing up files is to back up projects with all the elements that you need. This means archiving any logos, files, photos, fonts, and anything else that will help the project go smoothly if you ever need to access it again. What makes it really easy is the "collection process," or making a "package." Some programs, such as Adobe InDesign, collect the information for you and create a folder containing everything you need. I try to back up to an external hard drive at least once a month. Computers keep getting smaller and smaller. External hard drives are small, relatively inexpensive, and can hold a lot of information.

Another consideration with your computer is what screen size you prefer working with. If you are working with an older, small monitor, you will not get the same view as your client as they look at your logo. You don't necessarily need the biggest, most high-end computer monitor available but make sure you have a good one. Some designers have two or three flat-screen monitors lined up on their desk connected to their computer while working on projects. I've never found this necessary, but if you are working on various components of a design, it might be a consideration. In other words, if you are creating a logo and want to view it as you work on it on a web page, and a mocked up business card, and a flyer, it might be useful to you. I suppose I'm probably just not that multi-faceted.

Mac vs. PC

I have to say that I am an Apple fan. Always have been. I think the Windows environment has come a long way in terms of handling graphic programs. I am just a Mac fan and always will be. It's a great, user-friendly operating system. I haven't had any problems with my Mac desktop or laptop. It boils down to preference.

When it comes to Mac versus PC, do what you are comfortable with and can afford. Windows-based computers seem to be less expensive than Macs. The PC world may have come a long way in the graphic design industry, but Apple has always had an edge on design trends.

I think Apple does a great job within the world of design. It has always been ahead of the Windows environment with its user-friendly, sleek, out-of-the-box look. I like its graphics, color, and just plain cool looks. You may feel the same about the PC package. I have taught myself on the Apple environments. However, I, and you, could certainly adapt to either platform. The corporate business world and its systems tend to be PC-based. The creative world tends to be Apple-based. You will be fine using either.

Software Applications

You should select software applications based on what is most commonly used in the industry. Just as chefs need the right kitchen tools, designers need the right design tools. You need to have design applications. I am very partial to the Adobe Creative Suite. I prefer to buy the whole program rather than some watered-down version that gives me just a few highlights of what the program can do. It's like a tease. The companies put out these "short versions" of applications I pay top dollar for.

My advice is to do it right and buy the full program. Adobe Creative Suite comes with all the applications you will need for your graphic design business. Visit Adobe's website for more information (adobe.com). While we are on the subject, there is this thing called the "cloud." Adobe offers monthly subscriptions to the cloud, and you can have access to the applications you need. So instead of spending $1,800 to $2,400 on Adobe Creative Suite, you pay a monthly subscription to use the same applications.

As I mentioned earlier, technology is changing all the time. Adobe Creative Suite is a great example. Applications are among the tools you should continue to invest in as new technology becomes available. Now, that doesn't mean go out and buy the newest and best applications as soon as they hit the market. Most experts will say to wait because the applications can come with "bugs," and waiting allows the company that produced them to issue updates or to fix those troublesome bugs. For me, a general rule of thumb is to wait six months. Do you have to buy every upgrade? No. But once you get two or three versions away from the original, your application is outdated. This has happened to me. A client will contact me to do something, and to open their file, I need a newer version than what I have. It gets embarrassing when a client has a newer version than I do. It's something we designers have to deal with. Our most essential tools—the applications that we design in—are constantly changing. It is an expensive but necessary cost of being in the graphic design industry.

Printer

Here's a loaded question: "What kind of printer should I get for my office?" I favor an Epson. It's what I am used to, and I know the quality is there. The type of printer you have will determine the ink and paper you use. I only use Epson products. I choose my printer based on the ability to print 11 x 17 paper with bleeds, maybe even as big as 13 x 20. My printer is not used for mass production. It is used for high-quality proofs. It's not a copy machine or a printer I would use to print thirty or forty copies of one project. It isn't made for that.

Printer Worksheet

What will you be using it for? _____

How many ink cartridges will it take to run? _____

What size paper does it handle? _____

Can it print double-sided? _____

Is having the ability to print 11 x 17 or bigger important to you? _____

Do you have space for your printer? (You don't want to feel cramped.) _____

Does a local store, like Staples, carry your supplies? _____

(Sometimes stores offer discounts and coupons on the items you need. This can come in handy and save you some money, too.)

All printers are not made equal. When it comes to proofs, you need a high-quality printer, so I wouldn't skimp here. My first Epson printer was around $300, and it was a great investment. It gave me quality proofs, and color was accurate from screen to printer. I made sure to use Epson paper and ink. I veered off and started using cheap inkjet paper, and the difference in quality was huge. It didn't go through the machine very well. There were a lot of misfeeds, and the color on the cheap paper was not up to my standards. Of course, I felt bad, but I also felt that I should at least get through the ream I had bought. I grew increasingly frustrated and experienced more paper jams, so I stopped using the paper altogether. I became even more of a believer that you should use genuine products for your printer. I find that the Epson website has prices comparable to those of major retailers, and it runs specials with discounts or coupons. Printers are expensive to replace or ship out to fix, so why not use the products they were meant to run on? Your printer may last longer in the end.

All-in-One Printers

I do not have an all-in-one printer that includes a fax, scanner, and copier. Staples has made a lot of money from me because of that decision. You can get a pretty decent one for not a lot of money. However, remember my comment about keeping up with technology? All-in-one machines may be available at a reasonable price, but I would not recommend that you use one as your primary printer. I don't think the quality is there for printing proofs.

Still, an all-in-one can be a great add-on to your home office. If you don't think you will need one right away, hold off on buying it. With Internet and e-mail so widely used, fax machines are used less and less. I don't think they're going away altogether, though; faxing and scanning still come up in my routine.

Scanning has also come a long way. These all-in-one machines have some pretty decent scanners, too. A scanner can be a valuable addition to your equipment.

You will need a copier on almost a daily basis. When I started out, I was running to Staples all the time to make copies. The printer in my office is not made for multiple copies, nor do I want to use the high-quality Epson paper and ink to copy something. One page, not a big deal, but multiple copies are not cost-effective.

All-in-one printers have come a long way and, most importantly, have come down in price. Keep in mind you also need room for this equipment.

Internet and E-mail Browser

These days it's not just about creating great design projects; you also need the "information superhighway" to transfer files to your client. Thank goodness it came into existence. I remember the "good old days" when the only way to get a proof to a client was to hand-deliver or possibly fax it, but faxing isn't a good idea for a first color proof. The Internet and e-mail have made our design lives a lot easier. They are essential to your business. They are how we communicate. One thing that is cool about technology is you can check your e-mail and use the Internet on your smartphone. You have the ability to stay connected.

The Internet can be used in so many ways. It can be a great tool just for doing research for yourself or your clients. Make sure your Internet connection can handle big files. You will need to get to different websites to do your job. I would advise you not to stray from the task at hand by surfing the Internet or going on Facebook. You can easily get distracted and next thing you know, it's an hour later. Just as if you were in a corporate environment, you can't spend all day surfing the Internet and getting distracted from doing your job.

Using e-mail is a great way to send PDF proofs to clients, and they can safely look at the files on their end. Check with your local provider to ensure that your Internet and e-mail browser can handle large files.

Handling E-mails

One thing I need to caution you about is handling e-mails. Always be professional. Typing like you are texting is unprofessional. It doesn't matter what level you are on with your client; it's still business. Be professional in your correspondence, always! Don't let e-mail be your only form of communication. It's so easy to type an e-mail and get it out in a hurry, but go to the old-fashioned way of doing business and use the phone with a smile in your voice.

There are websites that can help with transferring big files. I use the Hightail site (hightail.com). It's a great way to get big files to your clients or even to commercial printers when you have an approved file. Dropbox (dropbox.com) is another very popular way to share large files.

Phone

With technology these days, people are doing without old-fashioned land lines. You can run your business using your cell phone and cell number, but I would advise having a land line in your office if you don't have a reliable signal all the time. It's embarrassing to have a conversation with a client who is saying, "Are you there? Hello? Can you hear me?"

Of course, cell phone calls can also drop when you're traveling, but I would recommend that you have your own business line. This will make you look more professional. If you share a household with children and a spouse, you don't want clients leaving messages on your home phone. You wouldn't want someone to question the legitimacy of your home-based business.

Supplies

As you can see, the list of what you need in your home office can get long. Supplies can mean anything—paper, ink, pencils, file folders, file cabinets, etc. Supply expenses can add up quickly, so be practical. Ink and paper for my printer are expensive. I use them sparingly and carefully. You need to keep up with supplies. I have, on occasion, run to the store in the middle of a project because I ran out of ink or paper. It may sound silly, but keep track of your supplies. Keep a list so you know when they are low, not out. Buy them when you are low so that when you need the supplies, you have them.

Good Lighting

You need to see things in close detail, so have good lighting in your office. If you are lucky enough to have windows, natural lighting will add to your atmosphere. Windows are great when you want to take a little break from the computer screen for a few minutes and turn off your head. However, make sure that the lighting is not creating a glare on your computer screen. It seems like a silly detail, but it's important.

Music

This is certainly a matter of preference, but I like having music on when I'm working. There are times when I like it quiet, but I feel I am more creative when I have music in the background. This is really up to you, but I like it. Just a bit of advice: Make sure your music isn't loud when you are taking a business call. Clients don't want to hear your music through the phone.

Are these items necessary all at once, before you have even opened your doors? No, but buy wisely and shop with clear priorities of what you need versus what you want.

04

Writing a Business Plan

Why You Need a Business Plan

Taking a trip without knowing where you are going may sound like fun to a lot of adventurers. Traveling without a map can indeed be fun—as long as you don't care where you end up. But as baseball great Yogi Berra once said, "If you don't know where you're going, you might not get there."

You should never start a business without having a plan of what you want to do and where you want to take the business. The consequences of a lack of planning can be devastating, both to you and to others who have trusted you.

A business plan does not need to be a monstrous tome with pages of speculative guesswork, graphs, and statistical charts to try to rationalize those speculations. A business plan should ultimately be your guide—your roadmap—which you can use to run your business the way you want to.

As a graphic designer, you may have a tendency to gussy up your business plan, even if it is just for your own benefit. If you find yourself creating a nice cover for it and becoming focused on the appearance of your plan, it may be time to take a step back and evaluate who you are making your plan for.

If you are getting financing from a formal lender, you may also need a business plan for the lender. You should consider creating two business plans.

THE IMPORTANCE OF PLANNING
by Jim Smith

Many years ago, when I first started running businesses, I felt like I didn't need a business plan. I treated my businesses capriciously—almost recklessly. It was a fun adventure. I didn't need to plan because I felt I knew what I was doing. And if all else failed, I'd just close up and go do something else.

However, the reality hit me hard the first time I had to close my doors. I had to tell my employees that I unexpectedly ran out of money. They thought they had a future with my business, and they were devastated. I had to tell my vendors—the companies that trusted me with products, assuming I was responsible enough to take that trust seriously—that I hit a bump in my business that I hadn't planned for. There was something horrible about my landlord putting up a CLOSED sign. I failed, and it was there for the world to see.

A lack of planning in business is not an exciting adventure; it is a thoughtless and inconsiderate way of setting yourself up for failure while dragging others along for your joyride. Don't treat your business like a gamble. You are risking more than your own future.

You need a nice, fancy plan, formatted professionally with content that your banker has requested. Make sure all your projections, while realistic and justifiable, are optimistic and confident. If the bank requests any charts or tables, it is time to use your design skills to impress them. But with the difficulty in getting financing today, it is hard to get lenders' attention.

If your parents or a successful sibling are willing to help you get started, they will likely want a less formal business plan, with more thought given to how you will achieve success in both the short term and the long haul. If you are just putting a business plan together for yourself, it can be as informal as you want. It is your roadmap to your success. Content matters.

Without a plan, the business runs you. Without a plan, your customers or competitors decide how much you should charge. You stumble into decisions, and you will ultimately realize that you are not in charge of your business. You don't even know what your business will look like without a plan.

How to Write the Business Plan

Your business plan should be developed in two phases—first is the fact-finding stage followed by an analysis of those facts. Gathering facts (congratulations, reading this book is part of that!) will require the most time. The analysis, while not as time-consuming, is still an integral component of creating a successful business plan. The tendency is to do some fact-finding, read a few books, talk to a graphic designer, and then plunge right into your new business without giving a hard look at the data you've accumulated.

Your fact-finding mission should certainly include these tasks:

- Read books on business as well as on graphic design.
- Read some blogs by other graphic designers, and perhaps even leave an occasional question or compliment in the comments section when appropriate.
- Join and become active in some online forums for graphic designers.
- Join or, if none are available in your area, set up a Meetup (meetup.com) group for local graphic designers.
- Meet one-on-one with other graphic designers. (Out-of-town designers are more apt to give out accurate information than local ones reluctant to help a competitor.)
- Meet related, but not competing, businesses such as printers, bulk mail companies, marketing gurus, sign companies, and even trade show organizers.

Structure of a Typical Business Plan

Introduction

Business Vision

This should be a broad overview of how you envision your business. It should only be a paragraph or two of summary. Many call this section an "elevator pitch"—a quick and intriguing description that you could deliver in a brief elevator ride.

Your Present Scenario

This is your starting point. Are you currently employed, laid off, or moonlighting as a graphic designer?

Your Skills and Credentials

Include in this section everything that contributes to your ability to become a successful graphic designer. Think of it as a mini résumé. Briefly describe where you work and how that work adds to your credibility. Have you earned any awards or diplomas? This is no time to be modest. Bring out all the reasons why you will become a great graphic designer.

Why You Will Succeed

Building upon your skills and credentials, briefly describe how you will use those talents to steamroll over your competition and make you the desired professional in your field.

Your Financial Status and Desires

There will be more opportunity below to provide details on your finances, but give an overview of your current financial situation and what you hope to accomplish in your business.

Goals or Milestones

You will need to discuss two things here. First, where would you like to be a year from now, and then five years from now? No pie-in-the-sky here. Give reasonable goals. Next, provide some realistic milestones you plan to achieve to attain those goals. Some important milestones to define include when you plan on starting your business. If you are currently working elsewhere, when do you plan on striking out on your own? (Make sure to mention that you will give plenty of notice to your job and any transitions.) If pertinent, include when you will graduate from school and start out on your own. Give some substantial milestones indicating that you have really thought this through and are not just another dreamer wishing to open your own business someday. Show that you are serious and know how you plan to get there.

About You

Your Primary Industry Skills

Again, this is not the time to be shy or modest. Define what skill set you bring to your business. Do you have any business experience? Did you orchestrate a successful fund-raising event for your favorite nonprofit? Start learning how to talk yourself up—that can help you succeed in the business world.

Your Main Weaknesses

Here you can bring your ego back to earth. But more important than just identifying the weaknesses that can hamper your success, what is your plan to overcome them? If you don't know how to do any bookkeeping, you might want to take a class on how to read a balance sheet and profit and loss statement. If you love to create designs but detest selling your wares, what will you do to overcome that? Bring in a partner who loves to sell? Or will you take classes at your local college on sales and marketing? Owning your own business will bring out weaknesses that you may not have realized you had. Showing that you have the ability to identify some of them—and, more important, confront and overcome them—is paramount to your ability to become and stay successful.

Your Graphic Design Services

Description of Your Services

In the chapter on envisioning your business, we talked about the vast array of services you can offer. Identify the services you plan to provide, with a bit of a description about each of those services and how they fit into your business.

Your Business Region

Where do you expect to conduct the major portion of your business? A Web designer can get work across the globe, as the work flow is all electronic. But if you provide brochures, flyers, and other printed materials like I do, you might want to plan your region to be local. Either way, make sure to identify your primary region in your plan.

How Your Services Get Delivered

This can be an overlooked detail, depending on what services you offer. If your graphics include large banners for fund-raisers, will you be driving those to your clients? Will all of your materials be electronic and sent via e-mail? (Remember that if you deal in print media, those files may be too large for e-mail.) Do you need a small delivery van for your graphic designs, and, if so, are you including that in your plan?

How You Plan to Beat Your Competition

If you feel that there is plenty of business for everyone or that you don't really have any competition, you should consider that thought carefully. There is rarely a successful business that does not have competition. And if there is not much competition, once you start making good money at it, others will jump in. So plan on having competition, and plan on how you will build your niche or carve out your share of that market.

Any Services You Plan to Add Later

As your business grows, do you plan to add more services? Are you planning to modify the services you offer over time?

The Graphic Design Market

Where the Market Is Today

Show that you have a realistic idea of where the market is for your services. If the economy in your area is poor, is there a market within that environment for your graphic design service? How will you use that to your advantage? Will you provide inexpensive flyers to small businesses to help them improve their bottom line? If the economy is strong in your region, how does that affect the marketability of graphic designs?

How You Will Handle Market Shifts

Whether you are a cartoonist or an industrial designer for manufacturers, explain how you will cope with a downturn in your market. Conversely, how will you handle things if there is a boom and your business experiences a sharp increase?

Where You Feel Your Niche Can Be

As a graphic designer, you should plan on at least one, and possibly more than one, niche within the industry. I work well with a local print shop creating rack cards for small and midsize businesses. Rack cards are those 4 x 9 brochures that fit nicely in racks at restaurants and other businesses. The printer and I provide a one-stop purchase for rack cards: I take care of the design, and the print shop provides the printing, all for one affordable price. What are you planning on as your niche? Graphic design for websites? Or even more-focused mobile websites that are "thumb-friendly"?

Where Your Clients Will Come From
This may seem insignificant, but it is likely that clients will not come flocking to you. You need to find out where those clients are before you can figure out how to get them to come to you.

Profile of a Typical Client
This is also known as your target market. Describe a typical client. If you already have some clients, you can use one as a case study. Otherwise, make one up. Perhaps your typical customer would be Sandra from Betty's Bonsai Boutique. Sandra handles the marketing materials for the boutique. She sends out monthly mailings and needs help with the layout and design, and she produces an annual report for the boutique for which she needs your cover design services. She also uses you to produce 1,500 door hangers each month for use during the busy season. Once you create this typical customer, explain how that customer can be used to build your business. Are you planning on getting and maintaining one hundred of these clients? Or is your typical client big enough that you only need a dozen of them to pay the bills?

Why Should a Customer Come to You?
This is an important question that you should have an answer for. "What makes you different from all the other graphic designers out there?" is a variation of this question. If you don't have a good answer, it is time for you to develop your own unique business image; otherwise, you will blend in with other hopeful graphic designers. Your customers want to hire someone they feel will be better than most. You need to figure out why you are that person.

Your Competition

Who Is Your Competition?
Some people think they will have no competition. Don't be one of those people. You will have competition. You will have other graphic designers who want to take your

business away from you and keep it for themselves. They may invite you to have a cup of coffee and pretend not to be competition. That is a nice gesture, but don't believe it. I meet competitors frequently. I run into them at chamber and networking events. I invite them to coffee or they invite me. I don't mind chatting with them about my business or asking about theirs. But I never forget that, unless they are hundreds of miles away, they may be trying to take my next client away from me. They may not know that I'm on the other side of that tug-of-war. They may not even know there is another graphic designer competing against them on that juicy proposal. But don't placate yourself into thinking you have no competitors.

How Well Do You Know Your Competition?

There is an often quoted line in *The Godfather: Part II*: "Keep your friends close but your enemies closer." This is very true in business with your competitors. Of course, for the most part, your competitors are not your enemies, but you want to keep an eye on them. You don't need to be hostile, nor do you want to isolate yourself from your competitors. When I first started out in business, I found opportunities to meet with other graphic designers nerve-racking. I've since learned that friendly competitors can share tips (much like I'm doing in this book) and, on occasion, even business. I was even given the opportunity to take over a competitor's clients when he went out of business. He got to know me well enough that when he wanted to jump back into the job market, he highly recommended me to several of his clients.

Are Other Services Your Competitors?

Don't assume that other graphic designers are your only competitors. Microsoft Word and other software programs took a lot of flyer and brochure work away from graphic designers. You may feel you can do a better job of laying out a brochure than a business owner with a software program (and you likely can!), but that business owner may not recognize that difference enough to pay for it. In that case, the software program has become your competitor. I was horrified when someone pointed out an online service called Fiverr (fiverr.com) to me. For five dollars my client can get someone to create a flyer, brochure, business card, caricature, logo, or other graphic design. Has that put me out of business? No, of course not. But it is a service that is in competition with me. You need to be aware of your competition and have a compelling reason why your client should stay with your services instead of shopping your competitors.

Promotional Planning

How You Plan to Promote Your Business

Make sure to include some specific promotional plans for your business. It is very unlikely that you will hang your shingle out and suddenly business will come running through your front door. You will need to promote yourself. There are numerous ways to do that, and we devote all of chapter 9 to many of those ways. But you will need to decide what works best for you and what will be the most effective way to bring in business. You can become active in your local chamber of commerce and attend various business networking meetings in your area. Your town probably has a local business association and would welcome a new local graphic designer as a member. I have found several networking groups in my area, including a very beneficial membership in the local Business Network International (BNI).

Advertising

How will you advertise your business? Will you have a website? Are you going to print some door hangers and go door to door looking for business? Will the Yellow Pages be part of your advertising spending?

Plans to Publicize Your Business

Depending on the focus of your graphic design business, you may find it helps to attend trade shows, local manufacturing shows, or even boutique gatherings. Think of places where your target market gathers and then try to get yourself an invitation. If your market will be local restaurants, perhaps you will want to attend the regional restaurant association convention. If your target market is construction contractors, find out when and where the home shows are in your area. Show up with a handful of your business cards and start learning about your market's graphic design needs.

Your Financial Plan

Pricing Structure

What do you plan to charge for your services? This is where you will outline your sources of revenue.

Start-up Financial Situation

Do you have a nest egg to help get your business started? A loan from a generous relative? A severance package from your former employer? Or are you completely broke and have a plan on how to hit the ground running so the money comes flooding in? If you have others putting money into your business, it is good to outline how you plan to sustain yourself while your new business develops a reliable stream of income.

Estimated Profit and Loss Statement

Most likely, you want your business to show a profit. But most businesses have so many moving parts that it is hard to tell what is profit and loss versus what is cash flow (covered in the next section). If you have a decent amount of cash in the business, you might think the business is profitable—even though there may be lingering bills that have not yet been paid this month.

Here is how to put a basic profit and loss (P&L) statement together in a spreadsheet. Compare the P&L statement to a cash flow projection, described below, so you understand the important differences. For a P&L, put twelve to twenty-four months across the top in column headings. For rows, start with a row called "Income," which is how much work you have invoiced, whether you got paid yet or not. Then list your bills ("Expenses") that have come in for the month, whether you have paid them or not. You might want to put them in categories if that is easier and then create a "Total Expenses" row to add them all together. Finally, calculate all your income for the month minus all your expenses. What is left is your profit or loss.

I have simplified the P&L to make sure you understand it. If you prefer, get your accountant involved, as there can be many more moving parts to your financial picture. Depending on how you have structured your organization (more on that later), do not forget to include your compensation (pay) for the work you do. Many people start their own business assuming they will just take some money as they need it and as the business can afford it. That is not a solid strategy for a successful business. If you do not include your pay in the plan, you may not get paid. And that is not a successful business plan!

Cash Flow Projection

Many people starting out in business mix up cash flow and profit. When you start your business, you might get a wonderful contract worth thousands of dollars. You jump in and start working, and, after a month of frenzied work, you suddenly realize you've done all this work and still don't have any money. It will take you a couple more months to complete the contract and get a check from the client, but you don't

Estimated Profit and Loss Statement

	Month 1	Month 2	Month 3	Month 4	Month 5	Month 6	Month 7	Month 8	Month 9	Month 10	Month 11	Month 12	Total
Income													
General graphic design	1000.00	1000.00	1200.00	1200.00	1200.00	1500.00	1500.00	1500.00	1800.00	1800.00	1800.00	1800.00	17300.00
Acme contracts	1200.00	600.00	1200.00	0.00	1200.00	600.00	0.00	1200.00	0.00	600.00	0.00	1200.00	7800.00
Bandara contracts	500.00	500.00	300.00	500.00	500.00	300.00	500.00	500.00	300.00	500.00	500.00	300.00	5200.00
Total Income	2700.00	2100.00	2700.00	1700.00	2900.00	2400.00	2000.00	3200.00	2100.00	2900.00	2300.00	3300.00	30300.00
Expenses													
Office rental	0	0	0	0	0	0	0	0	0	0	0	0	0.00
Advertising	20	20	24	24	24	30	30	30	36	36	36	36	346.00
Website	40	40	40	40	40	40	40	40	40	40	40	40	480.00
Internet connection	20	20	20	20	20	20	20	20	20	20	20	65	285.00
Cell phone service	80	80	80	80	80	80	80	80	80	80	80	80	960.00
Utilities	0	0	0	0	0	0	0	0	0	0	0	0	0.00
Auto mileage	25	25	25	25	25	25	25	25	25	25	25	25	300.00
iCloud online storage	0	0	0	40	0	0	0	0	0	0	0	0	40.00
Insurance	0	0	0	0	0	0	0	0	0	0	0	200	200.00
Periodicals	0	0	0	0	0	0	0	0	0	0	0	20	20.00
Bookkeeping	200	200	200	200	200	200	200	200	200	200	200	200	2400.00
Printing and postage	20	20	20	20	20	20	20	20	20	20	20	20	240.00
Owner's salary	2000	2000	2000	2000	2000	2000	2000	2000	2000	2000	2000	2000	24000.00
Health insurance	0	0	0	0	0	0	0	0	0	0	0	0	0.00
Taxes	50	50	50	50	50	50	50	50	50	50	50	50	600.00
Total Expenses	2455	2455	2459	2499	2459	2465	2465	2465	2471	2471	2471	2736	29871
Profit/(Loss)	245.00	(355.00)	241.00	(799.00)	441.00	(65.00)	(465.00)	735.00	(371.00)	429.00	(171.00)	564.00	429.00

	Month 1	Month 2	Month 3	Month 4	Month 5	Month 6	Month 7	Month 8	Month 9	Month 10	Month 11	Month 12	Total
Beginning Cash on Hand	2000	1395.00	550.00	1685.00	1416.00	1967.00	1118.00	1483.00	1728.00	1173.00	2132.00	2071.00	
Income													
General Graphic Design	0.00	1000.00	2000.00	1200.00	1200.00	1200.00	1500.00	1500.00	1500.00	1800.00	1800.00	1800.00	16500.00
Acme Contracts	0.00	0.00	1200.00	600.00	1200.00	0.00	1200.00	600.00	0.00	1200.00	0.00	600.00	6600.00
Bandara Contracts	0.00	500.00	300.00	500.00	500.00	300.00	500.00	500.00	300.00	500.00	500.00	300.00	4700.00
Loan from Aunt Nicky	2000.00	0.00	0.00	0.00	0.00	0.00	0.00	0.00	0.00	0.00	0.00	0.00	2000.00
Total Cash Coming In	2000.00	1500.00	3500.00	2300.00	2900.00	1500.00	3200.00	2600.00	1800.00	3500.00	2300.00	2700.00	27800.00
Payments													
Office rental	0	0	0	0	0	0	0	0	0	0	0	0	0.00
Advertising	0	20	40	24	24	24	30	30	30	36	36	36	330.00
Web site	120	0	0	120	0	0	120	0	0	120	0	0	480.00
Internet connection	60	0	0	60	0	0	60	0	0	60	0	0	240.00
Cell phone service	80	80	80	80	80	80	80	80	80	80	80	80	960.00
Utilities	0	0	0	0	0	0	0	0	0	0	0	0	0.00
Auto mileage	25	25	25	25	25	25	25	25	25	25	25	25	300.00
iCloud online storage	0	0	0	40	0	0	0	0	0	0	0	0	40.00
Insurance	0	0	0	0	0	0	0	0	0	0	0	200	200.00
Periodicals	0	0	0	0	0	0	0	0	0	0	0	20	20.00
Bookkeeping	0	200	200	200	200	200	200	200	200	200	200	200	2200.00
Printing and postage	20	20	20	20	20	20	20	20	20	20	20	20	240.00
Owner's salary	2000	2000	2000	2000	2000	2000	2000	2000	2000	2000	2000	2000	24000.00
Health Insurance	0	0	0	0	0	0	0	0	0	0	0	0	0.00
Taxes	300	0	0	0	0	0	300	0	0	0	0	0	600.00
Total Paid Out	2605	2345	2365	2569	2349	2349	2835	2355	2355	2541	2361	2581	29610
Ending Cash on Hand	1395.00	550.00	1685.00	1416.00	1967.00	1118.00	1483.00	1728.00	1173.00	2132.00	2071.00	2190.00	2190.00

have any money to pay bills until this comes in. But your P&L shows you are making a profit. You've just learned that you can have a profitable business but not enough cash in hand to sustain you.

To create a cash flow pro forma, take a spreadsheet and create columns for each month for at least a year, preferably two. The first row is your starting cash on hand. The second row itemizes all the money you will have coming in for the month. Remember that just because you invoice fifteen clients this month does not mean you have the money from those clients yet. This is a cash flow statement—not an income statement. For the next row, put all the money you will need to pay out this month. Finally, put the money you have on hand at the end of that month—your starting cash plus your money coming in for the month, and subtract the money you paid out this month. That total is how much cash you have at the end of the month. If that amount is below zero, how do you plan to make up the difference? Do the cash flow for each month to make sure you have enough cash reserves to make it through any lean times.

Running Your Business

The People
This is your human resources plan. For most of you, this is an easy task because you are the key person in your business—as well as the only person. Fine. Give a brief description of yourself as the sole person in your business. However, if you are planning on bringing in a partner, spouse, or others to help you, you need to identify those people, what their positions will be, and how they will be compensated for their work.

Business Structure
Your business will need to have some legally defined structure. There are several options to choose from. According to the Internal Revenue Service, the four most common types of business structure in the United States are sole proprietorship, partnership, C corporation, and S corporation. These are discussed in more detail in chapter 8, but here is a broad overview as well.

Sole proprietorship is just what it sounds like: You are the sole owner of the business. Most small businesses start out this way. A partnership is an agreement between two or more people to co-own a business. The partners can share equally in the responsibility and the profits, or these can be divided in a wide variety of ways. One of the big disadvantages to sole proprietorships and partnerships is that each person involved is equally responsible for the business. Any lawsuits or a failed business can put each person at risk for losing everything. These are easy business structures to set up, but be sure you get some legal advice before deciding what is best for your needs.

Structuring your business as a C corporation (known by many as a regular corporation) or as an S corporation gets complex. A corporation is a separate entity. You do not own a corporation; instead, you own stock in it. Even if you own all the stock in the corporation, you still don't own it. If someone sues your corporation for your actions, that person usually can't touch you directly as long as you've obeyed the corporation's bylaws. (Disclaimer: I'm not a lawyer, nor do I have space here to go into all the exceptions and variations in this basic discussion of corporations.)

The main difference between an S corporation and a C corporation is that a C corporation pays tax itself, whereas in an S corporation, the shareholders pay the taxes themselves. If you decide to set up a corporation, you will likely become president, CEO, or director. As president, you will direct your corporation to give the president (you) a raise or to accept a loan from you. Everything you do becomes separate from, and on behalf of, the corporation. You can't take money out of the corporation without getting prior permission from the corporation.

It may even start to sound silly that you are formally requesting that the corporation grants the shareholder a nice life insurance policy or other benefits when you are the only one involved. But if you try to take a loan out of the corporation without obtaining the required approvals, you are setting yourself up for some lawyer discovering that you did not follow the rules set forth in your corporation's bylaws. That lawyer will then declare that you don't really have a corporation and will, to use their expression, "pierce the corporate veil." With that, you've lost the protection provided to you as a corporation. Corporations are not to be taken lightly. You must follow the rules that you and your attorney have set up for your protection.

There is also a structure sanctioned by states called a limited liability corporation (LLC). In most states, the LLC limits your liability much like a C corporation, but the profits and taxes are handled much more like a sole proprietorship. You should talk with a small business accountant and attorney to learn about the pros and cons of each based upon your business and which state or country you are located in.

Client Satisfaction Policy

This is rarely put into a business plan, but it should be—it is an important aspect of your overall business strategy. No matter how hard you try, you will run into customers you just can't satisfy. How will you handle them? Will you force them to pay for the time you've put in regardless of whether or not they are happy? Will you include a clause in your contract that lets them give a partial payment? How you handle customer satisfaction, or a lack thereof, is entirely up to you, but it would be a good idea to have a plan in place before it happens.

Office

Because you are reading a book about your home-based business, I assume you will have your office in your home. But be more specific. Where in your home will your office be located? How big is it? Will you cordon it off from the rest of your house so you can get work done without family members or pets interrupting? This is all part of your business plan.

What to Do with Your Business Plan

What you do with your plan depends on where it is needed. If you are dealing with a banker or other formal lender, you will need a polished version of your business plan to present to them. This will be the plan that requires your skill as a graphic designer to make it both attractive and informative.

If you are creating a business plan for family members or close friends who will be entrusting you with some of their wealth, you want to win their trust with a plan that shows that you know not only how to be a graphic designer, but also how to run your own business successfully.

The majority of you will create the plan for the same reason I did—to make sure you have thought of everything and that you are capable of succeeding.

Whichever reason you are creating a plan, do not skimp on details and planning. General Dwight D. Eisenhower once said, "Plans are nothing. Planning is everything." He was planning on invading Normandy at the time. He knew that creating a plan is necessary, but bringing it to life by continuous planning is vital. Build your plan, but expect to enhance, develop, and modify it as you go. If sudden, unforeseen changes arise, having a well thought-out plan will allow you to make adjustments to your planning to stay on top.

A business plan should be a living entity. Like a road map, keep it and use it. But when it is time to take a detour in your business, you will have the structure in place to make any necessary zigzags while still allowing you to get your business back on track.

05

Getting Started

Planning Stages to Open for Business

Once you have come to the important decision of wanting to start your own business, well, how do you get there? How do you get to that all-important "open for business" day? This all depends on you and how badly you really want to get there.

The first step is to love what you do. As the old Confucius saying goes, "Choose a job you love, and you will never have to work a day in your life." If you love what you do, there is a tendency to work harder, stay motivated, and want to succeed. When I became self-employed, I discovered a real passion to strive for my best in owning my business. Not to mention, I was happier. When I lost my job, I was devastated. At first I was upset, mad at the world, wondering why me. The company called it "job elimination." I left on good terms, so I can use them as a reference. And I received a severance package.

But there was something missing. I now know that the thing that was missing was that I wasn't happy anymore. So when I ask if you love what you do, it is because that is half the battle. You will be happier. I think part of loving what you do and setting yourself apart from your competition involves thinking about the skills you like to use most. List them: strengths, expertise, knowledge of the industry, etc.—whatever makes you the best in your field. I want to add here, too, that it's not just professional skills; you bring to the table personal experiences as well as your communication style. These, in my opinion, are just as important.

With your business, tap into what you do well. This will help bring you the life you want. I also think it's important to have core values and principles that you can implement in your business. You should treat people how you want to be treated. As a business owner, your personal life and philosophy are important, as those often coincide with your business life. Keep your character and self-respect at the top of the list.

I know I am going to sound like a mother, but you need to plan in order to own your business. What are the right steps and in what order? Well, that is probably up to you. It seems like there are more and more businesses popping up in the community. Based on the economic times, with the job market so crazy and unpredictable, opening a home-based business seems to be a logical route to generate income.

In this book we are talking about graphic design, but wanting to have your own business, no matter what your core service is, takes guts and a lot of hard work. Anyone can start a business, but it's the few successful ones that put their nose to the grindstone, roll up their sleeves, and prepare themselves for the rocky road ahead. Make sure that you are ready for the twists and turns of owning your own business. Challenges and obstacles will test your patience and your drive. Self-doubt and worry might make you begin to waver. But when times are lean, really lean, and you ask yourself, "What am I doing owning my own business?," if you have that passion, you will find the strength and courage to meet those obstacles. There will be many challenges. Your unique style sets you apart from your competition. Believe me, there are plenty of graphic designers out there, and even other professions that incorporate graphic design into their business. Hold your head up high, for you have something special to offer.

I think the best way to put it is this: Be flexible. Adapt to change. Think about what you can improve on and where your strengths are in wanting to own a home-based business. Nobody is perfect. Remember that. There are many business owners out there that have been here in the beginning stages of starting up a business. Learn from them. Talk to the owners and probe their knowledge of what worked and what didn't.

I am flattered when someone asks me about how I started or wants my advice. If I can help steer someone in a direction that will be best for him or her, then by all means, I want to share my experience. I'm not perfect, but I am more than willing to share what I have learned along the way. When someone seeks you out for advice, there is an element of confidence that is sure to make you feel good. It is those moments along the way that make it all worth it. If you are determined, spunky, and fiercely independent, you are on the road to being a successful business owner.

> **Things to Consider in the Planning Stages**
>
> - Why do you want to own your business?
> - What are your goals for your business?
> - What skills will be needed to start, be successful, and continue to grow your business?
> - What will you start with as far as capital? More important, what do you need to make it and to survive?
> - Write your business plan (see previous chapter).
> - Research the competition.

First, plan, plan, plan. Organize your office. Have the tools you need to design. Make sure your computer is functional and that you have the latest graphic programs. You can network anytime, but it's crucial to start doing so as soon as you are able. It sounds silly since we are designers, but do you have a business card? Even if you don't have every detail ironed out, at least have a way someone can get in touch with you if needed. Remember, be professional. I am a big believer that you have to make a great first impression with your marketing materials. You have to look good because you are preaching that you will make your client look good, so don't do anything halfway. Have a phone number that works.

Name your business and, if necessary, get an attorney to help you with the legal aspects. I preferred to become an LLC (limited liability corporation) based upon the laws in my state. Is an LLC necessary to do business? No. But I wanted to be protected. When I was "freelancing," I went to networking events and businesses after hours. I had a business card that had my contact information. I grew tired of saying, "I freelance. I am a freelancer." I wanted to add more legitimacy to my endeavor, so I hired a lawyer, officially named the business, and became an LLC—hence my name, Hunter John Designs, LLC.

This didn't all happen at once. I was definitely networking and going to any event that I thought might gain me business exposure. I more or less freelanced for five months. In those five months, I networked and handled projects with kid gloves. After all, this could be future business. A month later the paperwork was completed and I was officially Hunter John Designs, LLC.

Chapter 9 is dedicated to networking and joining different organizations, so we will dive into that later. Networking is so important that it deserves its own chapter.

Naming Your Business

What you name your business is completely up to you; there is no wrong way or right way to go about it. I do know from experience that a named business is much better than just saying, "I freelance." Naming your business gives you credibility, legitimacy, and a sense that you are an official, stable business entity.

How My Company Got Its Name

I thought quite a bit about what my company name should be. When I freelanced for five months, I thought about various names for my business and tucked some away in my head. If I were to name a business, what should it sound like? Did it reflect my personality? Was it easy to remember? Would the name start conversation? The word "design" is so generic that it could refer to many different professions. There are a few things that are basic about me, and I wanted my business name to reflect those basics.

I love being a mom to my son, Hunter. I'm a beach person all the way, and I love golden retrievers. I toyed around with various names such as Ocean View Graphics, Black Point Creative Group, Hunter John Graphics, Hunter John Designs, or Golden Hues. I had my favorites, but I also sought help from my friends and colleagues. I sent a list of various business names and asked their opinion, and they gave me some great input. Most of my colleagues liked my suggestions, but I held on to Hunter John Designs. I am so passionate about being a mom, and my son means the world to me. I know it seems silly, but I just liked how it sounded. It sounds classy, easy to remember, and is a good conversation starter. I get asked all the time about my business name: "What's Hunter John Designs? How did you get the name?" It is in honor of my son, Hunter John.

The name should be unique and reflect your brand. Is it corporate or not corporate enough? Some people use their actual name, but because you are trying to set yourself apart from others in the industry, that may not have much impact. Along with naming your business, I would suggest doing some research into what names might be open and available to use. The more unique you are in the name you select, the less chance there is that you have duplicated someone else's business name. When you decide to register your business name, an attorney can help guide you in the right direction.

I once hired a plumbing company to fix a clogged pipe. The company I picked was named Anderson & Sons Plumbing. A family business sounded good to me. When the plumber came over and started working, I asked the young-ish plumber if he was the father or the son in the company. He laughed and said he was the plumber and his four-year-old son was the up-and-coming plumber in his business. I smiled when I realized that I had hired a plumber based partially on his name. If you don't think your name matters, ask my plumber!

Brand Identity

One component of graphic design is brand identity, which is one of the coaching services I offer to clients. Brand identity is the coordinated use of all the elements of your own brand, such as colors, logo, name, and symbol. The elements should all work together to distinguish your brand from your competition, and more importantly, give you brand identity with your target audience. As you move along with your growing business, you gain brand identity.

I coach my clients that they have to be consistent in using their own brand. You have to practice what you preach by having brand identity yourself as well. In terms of basic design theory, find out which colors will work best. Which colors will be cost-effective to reproduce, especially for promotional items? Just as you do this for your clients, you should also do it for your own business. You need to remind yourself to use all of these elements together, consistently, as the perception that you build in doing so adds to the strength of your identity.

Having been in the industry for a long time, I have seen over the years that it's my client base and my target audience that build my brand once I, the designer, get the word out. Brand identity will come from building your business. As you grow, maybe your brand will shift as you adapt to growth, economic challenges, and competition. In addition, your brand identity also grows with your reputation as you build trust and ethical practices. I'm sure in your personal life you prefer to do business with people you know and trust. The same goes for your clients. Stay consistent and keep your business relationships strong. It's an ongoing process. You want to protect your reputation throughout your business dealings.

Business Identity

Now that you have considered owning a home business and are ready to hang out that shingle, there is a need for business identity. I will assume you have figured out what type of business you want to be, whether a sole proprietorship, LLC, C corporation, or S corporation. Most likely what will pertain to you is a sole proprietorship or a limited liability corporation. I've included more information on the business entities in chapter 8, but please seek out legal advice on what is best for you and your company, as I'm not a lawyer.

Address and Phone Number

The next step is simply how will you list your address and phone number. Some people don't want their address listed in their advertising materials, especially if it's a home-based business. For example, on my business card, I don't list my address. (However, I do include my address on other materials.) One alternative is a private mailing company, such as a UPS store, or a PO box with the United States Post Office. The PO box is cost-effective, but it can make someone think that yours is not a legitimate business. Potential clients may also think that you are a really small business, not in business for the right reasons, or not fully established. Just keep in mind your budget and what will work best for you.

I have mentioned this before, but it bears repeating: You should have a business phone line. Whether it's a cell phone or a landline, you need a separate number from your home phone. It looks more professional. Fax numbers will all depend on how often you think you will need to send faxes. Internet and e-mail have made fax machines less important. I don't think they will become completely obsolete, though, so if you anticipate sending a lot of faxes, purchase a fax machine and get a dedicated phone line for it.

Business Checking Account

In my experience, you must have a separate business checking account for business expenditures only. Your accountant will most likely agree with me on that. If you need to pay yourself—and, as a business owner, you will—then you should have your own money go into a personal checking account. It is wise to keep the expenses separate.

Do your homework. Banks are highly competitive these days in trying to get your business. It's a trend for banks to want to do business with small business owners and support their community, so most of them offer business checking accounts now. You don't need all the bells and whistles. A standard or economy business account should suffice. Be careful of fees or minimum balance requirements. I find that the smaller local banks, not the corporate big names, have the best rates and want your business.

Let me also caution you here about gimmicks from banks wanting your business. They get you to sign on the line with no fees and awesome business account perks, only to have the fees added once you have been with them for a year. One bank wanted a $2,500 minimum daily balance. If I could keep $2,500 in my bank account after bills, I would be dancing in the streets. That was a very hard figure to keep up with, as I was still starting out and growing. I simply couldn't afford it.

Do your homework and ask what your colleagues have done. Talk to different local branches to see what they have to offer, and make an intelligent decision. After all, it is your money. One good thing as you establish your business is that your bank will get to know you and your needs. As soon as your income will support it and allow the spending, your local small bank relationship can lead to a business credit card or even business loans to help with the growth of your business.

Business Stationery

Once you have the doors open, any correspondence must look professional, including business stationery. If you were freelancing as you gained momentum toward having a business, you should have had stationery made already. The more you act like a business owner, the more people will respect you as a business owner. Any time you have contact with someone—whether you are creating quotes, invoices, a business letter, or a proposal—there should be consistency in your business stationery. Business cards, stationery, and envelopes should all bear the same image. And please don't use the free business cards from the Internet with ads on the back to buy free business cards!

Designing Your Logo

This goes hand in hand with brand and business identity. It probably makes sense that you design the logo first. A good rule of thumb is to keep it simple.

Simple means it should be easy to remember and easy to reproduce on other marketing materials. All logos should be designed in a vector art program. Don't use anything that would rasterize your file. Vector art files can easily be enlarged or reduced without losing quality. They are easy to edit as well. Rasterized files can cause problems, especially when you want to reproduce them.

I agonized over my logo. First, one good rule I stick by, and I tell this to my clients as well, is your logo is a springboard for all other marketing materials. I'm sure that you have run into people who have no idea what to do about getting a logo. If you start with your logo—fonts, colors, an image or symbol—and consistently use it, that will put you one step ahead of the competition. Some people get a business card made—and others go so far as having other marketing materials made—before deciding they should get a logo done a few months into their business.

Your logo is the most important design element because it's the foundation of all the marketing you will do moving forward. Business stationery, a website, brochures, flyers, posters, or trade show displays are just a few examples. I could go on, but you get the idea. As we design for our clients, the same guidelines are true for us designers. Logos are time-consuming and can get expensive in terms of billable time. We have to please ourselves.

With that in mind, you should spend just as much time on your own logo as you would for a client. I am very critical of my client work and even more critical of my own work. Because you are in the graphic design field, you might think, "Well, I can design for clients, so I can just sit down and whip out my own logo." But there is more to it than that.

Creating good marketing materials yourself is the first step in gaining a professional image. Put in as much time as you would for a client. Take a step back and look over your materials. Do they fit your image? Do they fit your style and message? Remember the rules of good branding and make sure the logo you are creating looks professional. Because you are a designer, you should be able to give your logo a smashing look and feel!

Business Goals and Objectives

What are your goals for your business? Let's first define what the word "goal" means. According to the Merriam-Webster dictionary, it is "the end toward

HOW I DESIGNED MY LOGO

I went through several versions until I landed on what is now my logo. I spent hours deciding which colors and fonts to use, until the logo finally did represent me and my corporate image. I started out with colors. I knew I wanted to incorporate the color purple, as I tend to gravitate towards purple in just about everything I do. I wanted to have a fun, carefree, whimsical, and unique logo. That's what us designers have to do—achieve being different.

I spent a lot of time pondering which fonts to use, too. Deciding between sans serif or serif, and coming up with something that is easy to read, as well as something that would stand out, all played a role in my decision. I used Britannic Medium and Light. I knew I wanted purple, and from there I introduced a blue in the cyan family. But before I got to this point, I probably came up with ten or eleven different versions. Not really happy with a particular one, I sent the file out to a few colleagues and asked their opinion on the logos. I received some really good feedback.

While waiting for their input, I went back to Adobe Illustrator and tried to come up with something else. I used the brush element and very nonchalantly drew what looked like the H and made the color black, and made the J. It hit me like a ton of bricks. This was the one! Hence, my logo was born.

which effort is directed"—in other words, something you are trying to do or achieve. An objective, as defined by Merriam-Webster, is "something toward which effort is directed; an aim, goal, or end of action." The two words, goal and objective, seem to go hand in hand. A goal, especially when written down, provides a springboard in the right direction. An objective is the path to that goal, which leads to success.

Just as you have goals for personal growth, you need goals for your business growth as well. These will be effective as long as you have a vision of how to accomplish them and the motivation to get there. Some questions you can use to create your own goals can be:

- How many new clients would you like per week? Per month?
- When will your website go live?
- How many networking meetings will you go to each week?
- How much money do you need to earn to make ends meet and to be successful?

Some objectives to achieve the above goals can be:

- To get two new clients a week, I will make eight calls a day from my prospect list.
- My website will go live in six months, on *[date]*.
- I will devote time to networking and go to three meetings a week.
- I will need to make $500 a week to meet my income needs.

You get the idea. Think about your own goals. I think it's important that they be intertwined with your business mission statement. Part of reaching these goals is to write them down. Writing them down gives you a sense of ownership and motivation to stick to your plan and direction—at least for the most part, anyway. Tape them up over your desk to continually remind yourself. It makes you accountable for your actions.

Now, your goals may change as you work through this crazy idea of owning your own business, but starting out with simple goals is a good start. Be realistic about your goals, and adapt as needed as you go. When you write them down, it adds a sense of ownership. A word of advice here is to be gentle with yourself. Don't beat yourself up if you don't meet your goals right away, and be reasonable with yourself if you need to tweak them as you go along. Being realistic is the key. Set your goals high enough to be a challenge, but not so high that they are impossible to attain.

Your goals may be much different from mine. Remember that running your own business certainly takes your own personality and style. It also takes your own unique goals. When I first started out, I had the trade show company to lean on for income. But I still had a goal to avoid any lulls in activity or clients and to never be too busy to turn business away.

I want to say something about mission statements. A mission statement gives your company purpose. Think of it as a commandment. Why do you exist as a company? A mission statement usually starts with a "To" statement, such as: "To give exceptional customer service and create excellent marketing materials to increase our clients' bottom line." Keep it short and sweet, memorable, and a reflection of your business.

Your objectives can be at various levels. Because you are the boss while juggling the other jobs you handle as a self-employed designer, your objectives will likely differ from mine. My objective as the owner would be different from the objective of a receptionist, for instance. Objectives don't necessarily involve money or income. Wanting to be a leader in customer service or a leader in the industry are more qualities than numeric objectives. Both are important, but they can't necessarily be measured. If your objective is to give great customer service, how will you obtain it? You can do so by setting an example. To give the impression of great customer service, you must do it. This is where you might wear another hat, as you are your own public relations guru. Your objective is to gain exposure without paying money for it and to advertise your company without buying ad space. Good public relations involve you, the owner, practicing what you preach. If you want to be known for customer service, then walk the walk and talk the talk.

Just as in life, your business path changes as you make decisions. As the economy and other businesses change, so does your business. Here's a good example. Many of us want to lose weight at some point, right? Let's say my goal is to lose twenty pounds by June 1, so I give myself a target to reach. My objective is that I will exercise thirty minutes a day. I will walk three miles twice a week and cut out sugar from my diet. You get the idea. While I am on my diet, what happens? I skip the walk, sneak in a candy bar. What happens to my goal? I don't get to trim those twenty pounds. So I adjust and try harder the next week. Finally, the weight starts coming off.

Do you see what happened? I set my goal, I made an objective to meet that goal, and then I got to celebrate when I reached it. As hard as we are on ourselves to get there, we should celebrate good results and reaching our goals. On the other hand, be gentle with yourself when you don't reach them. Figure out why, adjust, and redirect your map. The journey continues.

Along the way, goals and objectives somehow help you focus your time and effort. We are so used to deadlines with our clients. Meeting deadlines makes us look good. Well, the same principle applies to business goals: Deadlines make us look good, and keeping them makes us, as business owners, feel good. It's an old-fashioned "pat on the back." These types of feelings keep us motivated. By staying motivated, we successfully reach our goals, and things turn out the way we planned.

It is much easier said than done, but think positive. If you see that you are not going to reach your goal, talk it over with someone, confide in a friend, regain composure, and change what needs tweaking. Are you going to have crazy, pulling-your-hair-out bad days? Yes. Just as when something drags you down in your personal life, adjust, learn, and move on. You are good at what you do. Keep sailing in the right direction.

Website

Hold on to your hats, my readers: I did not have a website when I first started out. I don't know if I can say it hurt me not to have a website, but I sure made it my goal to get one after I got through my first year of running a business. The need and client requests for a website just kept growing. To be honest, it started getting embarrassing that I didn't have one. Well, can you guess what my goal was? I planned to have my website go live within six months. You can find more details on setting up a website in the marketing chapter. But suffice it to say that a website should be an early goal for your business.

Steps to Opening Your Business

Here are some steps for you that lay out the planning stages of opening for business:

1. Do your homework. You may have already made the decision to own your own business, or you are reading this book for help in making that decision.
2. Prepare your office and get your equipment up to par and running properly. Go one step at a time with this, unless you have a lot of money to use for start-up costs. Just get what you need; you can always add things as your business income allows it.
3. Determine how and where you want to meet your clients. Choose areas of town that are convenient to you both. Scout out nearby Starbucks or other coffee shops to see which ones are conducive to client meetings.
4. Have your own marketing materials. You need a good, professional business card that lists a functioning phone number.
5. Start networking. It is never too soon to get out and meet people. Network with colleagues, friends, and neighbors. Join various groups. See chapter 9 for more ideas.

6. You can start up a home business in no time. Be prepared. There are no days off when you are just starting out. Get out there and hit the pavement. Like I said earlier, owning your own business is not for the lazy or the unmotivated.

7. Some days will be dreadfully slow, and you will wonder where the business is. Other days will be crazy busy, and you will wish it would slow down. Then, when it does slow down, you will wish it would pick up again. It will. These are just the normal ups and downs of running your own business.

8. You will need some type of contract, quote, and invoice system. Don't wing it. Check out chapter 6 for more help with these.

9. Once you establish your own business and are ready to talk to people, ask yourself if your marketing materials—such as your logo, business card, business stationery, contract, quote, and invoice—will make a great first impression. You don't have to get too far ahead of yourself, but you should have drafts and tweak them as you move along. You have to brand yourself. Are you holding yourself to the same standards that you would offer your clients? Are you consistent with your message?

10. You are a business owner. I highly recommend naming your business and getting it registered in the state where you live. Follow the required state guidelines and those your attorney recommends.

11. As I mentioned previously, I did not have a website at first. I wanted to get some actual clients, projects, and testimonials behind me first. I recommend you get your website up at the beginning, as this is the expected practice nowadays. It's up to the individual, but either way, you will need a website sooner rather than later.

12. Get out and hit the pavement. Talk to people. Talk to old bosses. Talk to vendors you know in the industry. Join groups. I didn't advertise. What I mean by that is that I didn't buy space to advertise my company. Most of my business comes through word of mouth, networking, and being involved in different organizations.

13. Remember to be professional when you are out there selling your services. Being professional builds trust, reputation, and credibility. Ask yourself: Would you hire your company? It is important to protect your image and business every step of the way.

14. Lastly, you need to be ethical. We'll discuss that in detail in chapter 8.

Start-Up Expenses Worksheet

Item	Estimate	Real Cost
Laptop computer	$1,000–$2,500	
Printer	$100–$250	
Scanner	$100–$150	
Read/write CD-DVD	$50–$150	
Digital camera (with extra battery, memory)	$100–$300	
Smartphone	$100–$300	
Professional fees (attorney/accountant)	$500–$1,500	
Insurance (liability/property, etc.)	$0–$1,200	
Software (graphics, design)	$50–$2,000	
Printing (business cards, letterhead)	$20–$200	
File cabinet	$50–$100	
Office furniture	$0–$3,000	
Office supplies (blank CDs, pens, stapler, etc.)	$50–$300	
Licenses, permits, corporate filing fees	$50–$400	
Membership fees (chamber, BNI, etc.)	$400–$600	
Start-up advertising	$0–$1,000	
Other		

Operating Expenses Worksheet

Item	Estimate	Real Cost
Office space	$0–$1,500/month	
Advertising (percent of desired sales)	2–4 percent	
Web hosting and domain name	$40–$50/month	
Internet connection	$30–$50/month	
Phone and/or cell phone service	$30–$60/month	
Electricity and other utilities	$0–$100/month	
Auto mileage or parking and expenses	$10–$200/month	
iCloud or other online storage	$0–$200/year	
Insurance	$30–$200/month	
Periodicals	$0–$50/year	
Bookkeeping/accounting	$50–$200/month	
Printing and postage	$25–$100/month	
Your salary (don't forget this one!)	$1,000–$5,000/month	
Health insurance	$0–$500/month	
Personal income tax, FICA, etc.	$0–??	
Other		

06

Show Me the Money

Starting your business is exciting, and the opportunity to be your own boss—well, that just takes the cake, right? Going from a steady income to "Who knows if I will get paid?" is scary, though. I would encourage you to talk to your friends and colleagues about what it took financially to start their own business. I strongly recommend that, before you tell your employer you are leaving, you weigh your options and assess how much money you have available to strike out on your own.

You have most likely put much thought into this decision to start your business. In my case, for the other half of my life, I was staying at home most of the time to take care of my parents, anyway. Had I not been in that position, I am not sure I would have been able to start my business. Times got so lean in the early days of my business that I wasn't sure how I was going to pay my next bill. Let's just say that there were some sleepless nights.

The best advice I can give you is to make sure you have enough money to cover your expenses for at least six months, if not more, when you are first starting out. Following are suggestions on how to protect yourself and prevent some sleepless nights:

- As we discussed in the previous chapter, have your own business checking account. Keep your business and personal finances separate. Once you establish a strong income and payment history, it's a good idea to get a business credit card. If you stay current and have good credit, there might be small business loans available, too, but I wouldn't base a business plan around that possibility, because it is not a strong likelihood in today's economy.

- Depending on which state you are operating in, contact your local government. The secretary of state usually handles small business issues and concerns. Rules and regulations for home-based businesses can vary from state to state.

- Put aside six to eight months, maybe even a year, of savings to cover your bills, business expenses, and personal obligations. Believe me, it gets tight and extremely difficult to stay afloat when you first start out. It's not all a joy ride. You will have lean times.

- Get advice from an accountant and a bookkeeper about your tax returns. Financial information can get tricky for businesses. You don't want to be caught off guard. Depending on your state or country, there could be sales taxes, value-added taxes (VAT), business entity taxes, annual filing fees, quarterly estimated taxes, or self-employment taxes. These are just a few expenses that you have to keep track of and whose payments you must schedule on time. Just your taxes and other state and local requirements can add up, and that's not including the daily expenses of running your business. There are software programs that you can buy to do it yourself, such as QuickBooks or TurboTax. Microsoft Excel is a good starting point for a business spreadsheet and to track your expenses and income.

- Inquire about business insurance. You are probably wondering why a graphic designer needs business insurance. Believe me, I was right there with you, asking that same question. Business insurance is similar to car insurance: We have it to protect ourselves. We pay the premium in case we need it and, boy, are we glad we have insurance if the unexpected happens.

- It is possible that your homeowner's insurance will give you the coverage that you need, but check with your insurance agent to see what is recommended. If you don't trust your agent to give you the honest scoop on what you need, shop around a bit to keep her honest! Look into add-ons to your current policy (add-ons in insurance jargon are known as riders or endorsements). A liability policy or a liability rider should not be too expensive. If you lease office space, frequently the landlord will require proof of liability insurance. If you go for larger contracts, you may be required to obtain an errors and omissions policy (also known as professional liability or E&O). That is rather pricey and is primarily obtained when a contract requires it.

- Of course, your policy could differ from mine, but ask about business interruption insurance. Without power, after all, you can't work. The premiums for basic coverage are relatively inexpensive for major peace of mind, so talk to your local insurance agent.

THOUGHTS ON BUSINESS INTERRUPTION INSURANCE

The weather has been entering uncharted territory. Big storms are more common. With big storms, your chances of losing power are greater. When I first started out, I didn't have a laptop. My home base was my desktop. When we lost power, I was out of luck and out of commission until the power went back on. One storm knocked out the power for nine or ten days in our metro area. For the self-employed, that seemed like an eternity. It wasn't just the nine or ten days without power; it was at least two weeks by the time I rescheduled my appointments, got back on track, and felt like myself again. Ten consecutive days without power will take a toll on you physically, mentally, and emotionally.

I learned after the storm that I could have put a rider (add-on) on my business insurance for business interruption for around $50 per year. That extra level of comfort is worth having a conversation with your insurance agent about.

One agent I talked with dampened my post-storm enthusiasm for the purchase of a business interruption rider. He pointed out that after our big storm, many small businesses did not get very much, if any, payout. He said that unless you have a storefront with a lot of traffic, it is difficult to prove that you would have gotten much more income anyway. So have a frank discussion with your agent. For me, the peace of mind is worth a few dollars, but you need to gather the details and make your own decision.

Pricing Goods and Services

Next you ask the two most important questions: "What am I worth?" and "What should I charge?" Before you have a client actually buying your services, you need to be practical about your rates. If your business is going through a slump, should you raise your hourly rate? No! Then you would be in a bigger slump. So the question becomes whether you should charge by the hour or charge a flat fee for a project. While I can't give you a magic formula that will make it clear what you should charge, what I can give you are some rules of thumb to help you make that decision. Just remember that a variety of factors and even the location of your business go into determining what you might charge.

Hourly Rates

First of all, be fair. If you want to charge $125 an hour, consider whether or not this is a reasonable rate. You may think that this would be a nice round number to work with, but what is your competition doing? What are the going rates for your area? Keep in mind, too, that with full-time employment you get a lot of perks, paid vacations, benefits, 401(k), or overtime pay. When you are self-employed, you have to factor all of those perks into the price.

Let me give you a word of caution here: Don't undervalue yourself. Conversely, don't have such a big ego that you price yourself out of business. I would like to get top dollar every time I talk with a client and thousands for every project, but that's not reality. You have to be fair and honest, but most of all you have to value yourself and your business. After all, you decided to work for yourself. You must feel you have something to offer and you are good at it. Put value on your business, yourself, and your talents.

Hourly rates come in handy and work with certain clients. When you are working as an independent contractor, an hourly rate is best. That negotiated hourly rate with someone who is going to mark your cost up to their client is usually less than if you are dealing directly with a regular client. For instance, I worked with a trade show and display company. They hired me as an independent contractor instead of full time, and they outsourced various projects to me. It was a great company and they had some great clients. The negotiated hourly rate was lower than what I would normally charge because the company marked my work up and resold it to their client. For example, a company might want to hire you to do some design work for a client at $40 an hour, even though your normal hourly rate is $65. You probably wouldn't be able to say, "I'll be glad to do it, but I need to get $65 per hour." You have to work for a lower rate so that the company can mark it up and make money as well. It can work to your advantage. This particular trade show company funneled me a lot of projects, so it was a win-win situation. I gained a lot of experience with large-format printing and designing large displays.

When you are working directly with a client and there is no other company involved, then bill at your normal hourly rate. When working with other companies for whom a lower hourly rate doesn't seem like a financially good decision, weigh the advantages. Will the company send you work on a frequent basis? Can the company be used as a reference? References are really important when you are starting out as a self-employed designer. The company could also do the best thing possible for you, which is referring you by word of mouth. So as much as you are thinking that hourly rates seem low and not worth your while, they can be very advantageous in the long run.

Don't sell yourself short. There will be times to stick to your guns and be firm about your hourly rate. Once you gain experience and have built a reputation with the company, you can increase your rate. When raising your rate, do it professionally and as an economically sound decision. Think of the company you are working with as a partner of sorts. It deserves to make money as much as you do. If the company doesn't make a profit off your work, it won't hire you again. So negotiate a deal that will be good for you and for the company. Once a company sees that you are looking out for its best interests as well as your own, it will be more likely to want to help you become more successful as well. It should be a win-win situation.

There are times when an hourly rate is simply better than a flat fee; for instance, when a client comes back and wants to make changes to an existing file or wants files burned onto a CD. The situation varies depending on the project.

Whether it's hourly or a flat fee, keep track of the hours. This will help you judge how long a similar project will take in the future and will keep you from unintentionally underestimating or overestimating your jobs.

Flat Fees

In my experience, a flat fee works best. I don't throw a number out there and think, "Yeah, that's about right." I really put some thought into how long the work will take me. How much research time will I need for stock images? How much time do I need for revisions? Is the client supplying the photos, logos, or text? Text is a big one. If it's a design from an existing marketing piece, the client might have the original file. If not, the text will need to be entered. Meeting with clients is also part of your time, and that time all adds up.

I list the various steps it takes to complete the job for the client and then show a flat fee. I keep "extra fees" separate and itemized, such as stock photos, sales tax, purchasing of fonts, and other items. Always plan and display all fees up front. If, for some reason, something comes up that you weren't expecting, be sure to communicate that to the client. Let's say you are working on a brochure, and the photos supplied by the client are not of the resolution or quality that you need for printing. Communicate to the client that the photos are not high-quality enough and suggest bringing in a professional photographer, buying stock photos, or having the client submit new photos. Photos are one part of the design that can make or break the look you are trying to achieve. The average businessperson doesn't understand our design world, including image resolution and quality, or even just selecting the right photo to depict the focused message.

What I am trying to point out is that as much as you prepare for the project or estimate the cost, detours can come up. Always be honest and explain these situations to your client. Whether you are estimating with an hourly rate or flat fee, try your best to be on target and to charge a fair price.

Part of your cost includes revisions. This can come back to bite you if you are not careful. I don't charge for revisions. So far, it's worked. I also say up front that the number of revisions can't be taken for granted and that the revisions must be within reason. Many competitors charge for revisions after a fair amount up front. Let's say your project allows for three sets of revisions, and you are on your eighth round. If you have a client going off track in this manner, it's up to you to rein them back in. When clients intentionally or unintentionally keep asking for one small change after another, or one small add-on after another, it is known in the industry as "project creep." It happens to everyone who deals with these types of projects, as you will learn along the way.

If you keep great records and track your time, you can judge whether or not you are giving your client a fair price while still making money. Part of the process is to keep in mind the expense it takes to make a job complete, besides the obvious. Supplies, ink, paper, and assembling proofs should all factor into the equation.

Determining Your Rate

In figuring out your rate, you can do a little investigating. Use the Internet for comparable salaries, hourly pay, and experience level. Keep in mind your location. If you are in a small town, you probably would not be able to charge the same rate as someone living in New York City. Also keep in mind that you have to stay reputable with your clients. You can't charge different clients for the same work at different rates. That will come back to bite you. You never know how it might come up in conversation. If people start talking about who was charged what, you won't be in a good position.

This is where being fair and honest comes into play. Keep in mind that everything has to be factored into your rate: supplies and equipment, time, travel, buying stock photos, research time, and being realistic about what your time costs. Be consistent with your pricing. Not every project demands the same amount of attention and time. But be consistent. If you are charging hourly, make sure you keep track of your time (including proof assembly time) as you move through your project. If it took ten hours, prove those ten hours and be realistic about it.

Personally, I prefer using the "flat fee" quote. Most clients don't understand the time it takes to truly design from concept to draft or proof, revisions, and final approval. I itemize the project but don't necessarily factor in how long it will take. This leaves me a little breathing room if I need it.

Working within Your Client's Budget

Once you have established your reputation, the issue of the cost for your services won't be as much of a factor as it was in the beginning. When you first start out, your fees will be questioned and you will feel compelled to justify them. If you charge more than the client wants to pay, you will need to deal with that. However, if your rate is much lower than other designers the client has used, you may give the impression that you are offering low-quality services or are desperate for work. Finding that sweet spot between too high and too low will take some time and experience. The key is to position yourself as a professional but also a friend; you are trying to help solve clients' problems so they can make the best decision (hopefully to hire you!). Following are some ideas for dealing with price objections while you establish your reputation.

When a Quote Is More Than Expected

If you quote a client for a job and they balk at the cost, don't panic. Start asking questions. "Why do you feel my price is out of line?" is a good starting point for discussion. The surprise response would be if the client says that the price is so much lower than they expected. That is why it is best to ask questions rather than starting in on why your price is high—it might not be! I'll cover the lowballed quote in the next section, but let's assume the client is upset that the price is too high.

When you ask why the quoted price is out of line, you will learn what the client is basing that upon. If they just bemoan that the price is too high without giving you any more information, probe further. "I understand you feel it is high. What do you base that on?" Listen carefully and empathetically, as you are about to be given the key to saving this client. Here are the main reasons I've found that clients feel a quote is too high.

"I'm on a budget that can't be moved."

Treat this client as a trusted friend. Try to help them overcome this obstacle. First ask what they have budgeted for this project. They may be reluctant to tell you what they budgeted, but many times they will if you ask. Whether they give you an amount or not, explore ways together to lower the cost—less work, lower cost of paper, etc. This can sometimes uncover a solution; they may decide that perhaps the budget could have some flexibility to keep all the benefits of the project in place. Or if the budget is going to be revised soon because it is the end of the term, suggest requesting an increase for this project for the next budget cycle. Just keep in mind that you are trying to bond with your contact person to solve the budget problem. Dropping your price should only be an option if you have explored all other options and are willing to take a cut in pay this time. Be careful when doing that, however, because you may be setting yourself up for the client to haggle on every project in the future. I try to avoid dropping my price once I've quoted it, but you may try it as a last-ditch effort to save the deal.

"It is more than I thought it would be."

Ask some more questions. "What do you base that on?" is a good opener. If they say they got other quotes that were substantially lower, find out if those other quotes were for the exact same project. Wonder aloud why the other designers would be so much cheaper. I've been pleasantly surprised when a client will tell me why—for instance, the other quote is from a part-time designer in high school. Or, the CEO doesn't want to use the other designer and that is why they are getting other quotes. Asking questions can get you some amazing responses that will help you sell yourself. Just avoid sounding defensive, and mentally keep yourself on their side of the discussion. It should be the client and you working together to resolve this concern, never you against the client to push them into it.

"You are starting out and shouldn't charge that much."
I tried to avoid letting clients know when I was first starting my business. It gave them the impression that I should be much cheaper than everyone else and that I would work for any price just to get some business under my belt. But chances are that, even though your price is less than someone with much more experience and a better reputation, you've already set your price to be competitive with those other graphic designers. Just cheerfully agree with the client that they should get a deal, and that is just what you gave them. You gave them a break because you want to provide excellent service that will compel them to go out and tell others what a great job you did at a reasonable rate. But make the client promise not to discuss the great deal you are giving them with other potential clients, because that price is just for them. Assure them that you will be using their job as a showpiece for others because you appreciate their helping you get started.

"It just seems like a lot of money."
There are times when a client will complain about the price, but no amount of questioning will get them to divulge why the price seems unreasonable. This is likely a client who just wants to see if you will drop your price. Once you have explained that you have given them a good price and have stated all the reasons why you are the best person for the job, if you find there is no cooperation on their part, it may be time to smile, thank them for their time, and allow them to think about it. Once in a while, this may lead to a more fruitful discussion, but most likely not. Most of the time, these clients will not pan out and you'll never hear from them again. Sometimes I find out much later why I was up against a stone wall. I quoted one client only to have her declare bankruptcy a few months later. Thank goodness she didn't want to do business with me! Another time I found out through the grapevine that

it was the marketing person's nephew, a budding graphic designer, who got the job. Don't lose any sleep over those jobs that just aren't meant to happen. Keep looking for the clients who want your services instead.

When a Quote Is Less Than Expected

We've talked about high quotes, but there is also a danger of cheapening your reputation by giving a low quote. One of my larger potential accounts was with a former client who had already successfully used my services. He needed a major design overhaul, and I was the perfect person for it. He knew me, he was happy with my talents, and he was giving me a chance to bid on this large job. I bid low, knowing it would put a feather in my cap. I wanted to make sure no one underbid me.

I submitted my bid and waited two weeks for his decision. He contacted me and asked to meet with me to go over the details of the bid. When we sat down, he asked if I understood the extent of his RFP (request for proposal). I went through it step by step to show him that I grasped what he needed. He sat back with a disappointed look on his face and asked the crushing question: "Why is it that there are two very good finalists in this decision, yet you are bidding less than half of what the other guy quoted?" First, I was shocked that someone else would bid over twice what I knew I could do it for. I reminded the client that he had used my services before, and he knew that I always gave a fair price and never overcharged him. I told him that I wanted to win this bid and that was the reason I cut my rate for this project. He still was obviously nervous about the low price that I was quoting. I jokingly offered to increase the amount of my quote if that would make the task easier. Of course, that didn't help move the conversation along.

He told me that both designers had a proven track record and good reputations, and he would be happy with either. But the fact that I was giving him such a good deal really worried him. I reviewed all the reasons why he should be willing to give the contract to me. He then thanked me and said he'd make his decision in a couple of days. I left his office regretting my strategy of giving him a very low price to try to land the job.

In the end, the other designer got the job and I learned a painful lesson: Try to bid your jobs at just the right amount. No special deals to impress clients and no higher prices to try to make more on a client who may be able to afford it.

Prices for Nonprofits and Associations

Nonprofit organizations are often worthy charities that live on special donations at fund-raising events. They are always looking for ways to cut costs and to get services donated. Resources to pay for a graphic designer's services are typically stretched very thin. Trade and business associations are also working on a shoe-string but are funded differently. They are generally funded by membership drives and by advertising deals with their members. When the garage door opener association (yes, there is such a group!) wants more money, it needs to either wait for the next membership renewals or promote affiliated services in exchange for advertising revenue.

When I first started out, I felt that these were two groups that typically needed lower prices than others. Most of my competitors would steer clear of nonprofit organizations and business associations because they never had the money to pay well for services. Then I discovered there were some service providers who loved working with these two groups. So I started delving deeper into the reason why some designers do better with nonprofits and associations than others. Here is what I learned.

Nonprofits

A nonprofit organization does not necessarily mean a broke organization. Most nonprofits are very good at asking for favors such as free services. But they also realize that good businesses deserve to be paid for their services. They work their way through this apparent dichotomy by getting free services when they can and paying for the rest. But the key to working well with nonprofits is to know when they have funding and when they do not. Just because they recently completed a successful auction or golf tournament to improve their financial picture does not mean they can spend the money yet. They need to go through a budget cycle that allocates these funds. In working with a nonprofit, I have no problem asking when the funding will be available for the project they need.

Anyone who can approve expenditures also knows when the ebb and flow of money runs through the organization. When a budget cycle is coming to a close, that is the time to ask if they can add expenditures for your project. Otherwise, most of their money has already been spoken for.

The one exception to this is when fund-raising events come up. If you can prove that your cleverly designed banners will increase their revenue for their upcoming auction or telethon, the money can usually be pried from somewhere else. But this is not the normal flow of funds and can involve difficult red tape. If dealing with nonprofits, discuss the budget cycles with your contact person and work together to plan in advance for any design needs.

Associations

For just about any trade and professional services you can think of, there is an association eager to help them in exchange for some membership fees. In addition to many national organizations, there are frequently state associations under them and even local associations for larger groups. I was amazed when I learned how pervasive associations are.

But even the Association for Dressings and Sauces may need a graphic designer to help raise public awareness for its annual National Salad Head Competition at schools. If you can network with a decision maker in the association, you can likely build up some recurring business.

You will need to think the way the association does. You need to think of ways to help the association increase its revenue or its visibility to existing and potential members. Once you do your homework and know you can help them, try to assist with a smaller project just to get some exposure. Then ask how you can help with other events. Once you build that trust, you will become the expert on designs for the dressings and sauces industry.

Associations are not a fast, easy job for you. You need some insiders to help you help them, and you need to take the time to learn about the association, its goals and mission, when its big events occur, and even more important, when they start budgeting for these events and how you can become part of that cycle. So let them know you are in it for the long haul and available to help them whenever they are ready.

Working for Free

When we discuss working within a client's budget, we may as well include the client who wants or expects free (or almost free) services. After all, it is your favorite charity or your uncle's business, and it doesn't cost you anything but time to sketch out a flyer for them. And besides, think of all the great publicity you will get for doing it!

I used to get approached frequently to do free work with the promise of great exposure in return. I could get my name in front of a powerful board of directors for a substantial charity organization. Think of the exposure! However, I've learned a few reasons to avoid giving away my services.

Is that really all I am worth?

When an organization or business wants you to work for free with the promise of great exposure, just remember that they offer that same great deal to others. They are likely known for being tightfisted and looking for a handout. They may try to talk you into working for free while touting your wonderful services. But others who know them will also assume that you are desperate enough to do work for free. I gave away services when starting out to a well-respected businessman with the promise of lots of introductions. I actually got a couple of potential clients inquiring about my design services. But both wanted free services in exchange for more publicity. They figured out that because I had done such a spectacular showpiece for this business owner, I was desperate and willing to work for little money and many promises. And I guess they were right. But that changed in a hurry when I realized the real message I was sending out.

Busy, successful graphic designers may do some work pro bono (free) for a worthy organization, but they never do it expecting a return other than good feelings. They know what they are worth, and they charge what they are worth. And when they donate time to someone, it is a valued donation; it is not a veiled attempt at getting some free publicity. Of course, in giving some services away, they will get more back in good feelings. Their generosity may even bring in a grateful client or two. But never make that your motive for donating services.

How can we both benefit?

It is not easy to say no to your favorite charity or chiseling uncle who feels he deserves your talents in exchange for some publicity. There might be a lot of pressure to take on this "great opportunity" to design their event's brochure in exchange for a free ad. Here is a strategy that works for me: "If it is such a great deal for which I'm going to reap the rewards, let's set it up so we both win. You pay me my fair market value for my services, and every time I get a new client because of that little tiny ad that you let me put in your brochure, I'll give you a 10 percent referral fee for that sale." Then give the client plenty of room to backpedal.

That client is no longer convinced that this is something you can't possibly lose with because you are making them prove it. I've done this many times, and only once did I have it turn into a job for which I got a couple of signed contracts. Most of the time, you will learn that the client's "sure deal" starts unraveling before your eyes. And that is fine. I don't blame people on a tight budget for trying to get free services, but they won't get them from me. I needed all the paying jobs I could get when I was starting out. No free deals, thank you!

Double Your Rate

When you've been in business for a while, you will find some competitors who charge huge amounts—and get away with it! I used to get all self-righteous and full of indignation over it. I knew these designers were not worth twice what I was. But it never occurred to me that perhaps their rates were correct and I was underselling myself.

I was discussing this with a business friend who made me an uncomfortable proposition. "That's all you charge? Why not pick a good job coming up and charge twice what your normal rate is?" I immediately became defensive. "I could never do that," I said. "Why not?" was his quick challenge. The idea seemed preposterous. How could I ever charge double what my normal rate is? Even thinking about it was pushing me to the edge of credibility. I began to sweat at just the idea of it.

What would happen? Would the client ridicule me? The more I tried to talk myself out of it, the more intrigued I became with the idea. And an interesting transformation started happening: I began to justify the higher rate. Once I set my mind to charge more, I thought of all the reasons why it was reasonable.

I had a potential large client who needed a lot of hand-holding on a big project for me to bid on. I charged more than I ever had before—over double what I normally charged. I knew I was worth it, and I knew the client knew I was good. The question was only whether the client would realize I was worth as much as I had quoted for the project. A couple of weeks later when I got the good news of an approved contract, I was elated. I had taken a few steps up in my business. It was a good feeling. And maybe you will have a business associate who prods you to take your business to a new level someday when you are deserving.

Of course, I don't suggest you double your rates all the time. That will get you out of business in a hurry! But if you hear clients mention that your rates are very good, it might be time to give yourself a raise. A test you could use is to look back at your proposals and see how many of them were turned down because your quote was too high. If you seldom or never hear that, it might be time to increase your rate. Or if, like me, you need to shock yourself out of your current lowballed quotes, double your rate once or twice to see what happens. Scary, huh? Are you brave enough to try it?

Stock Photos, Professional Photography, or Client-Supplied Photos

If a design project includes photos, and most likely it will, be sure to include this in your quote. Buying stock images can get expensive, especially if you are purchasing the photos up front and not getting paid for them until the project is finished. The process of buying stock photos on various industry websites is easier, but they can get expensive depending on size, resolution, royalty rights, and how much they are per credit. Do your homework. Let the client know the cost per image. You may spend a lot of time researching images. Make sure you incorporate that time into the quote.

There are several professional photographers within my circle of colleagues, and I bring them into the fold when necessary. I can either build the cost into the price or have the client deal with the photographer directly. Either way, there will be times when working with a professional photographer is necessary. Choose yours wisely, as the photographer represents part of your company. Make sure you know the person well and that he or she is professional. Ask to see a portfolio.

The most cost-effective option is for clients to supply their own pictures, or to have them research the photo websites, buy the photos themselves, and then send them to you. Make sure they understand the minimum pixel size you need; otherwise, they may purchase the cheapest ones at a lower resolution than you need. It is critical that the proper photography be used in your project.

Communication

Sometimes the project will take unexpected twists and turns. I highly recommend that you keep the client abreast of your project. Maintain open communication with them so there are not any surprises. If you see the project drifting off track, bring it back in focus. If you feel that changes are adding cost to a project, speak to your client. Let the person or company know how the project is going so there aren't any surprises, especially when it comes to cost and exceeding your quote.

Sometimes you have to bite the bullet and suck it up. You learn to deal with these situations on a case-by-case basis. Just be candid with your client if you must change your original quote.

Open communication is so important. This includes follow-up. If you are waiting on text or a new photo from your client and some time has passed, maybe a week, call the client to find out where the missing parts are. Let the client know that this needs immediate attention or it could compromise the deadlines. Even if a passed deadline is the fault of the client, if it gets critical, you will likely be blamed for their slow response. Deadlines are critical to the project; don't let them slide too much.

What Is Your Break-Even Point?

Sure, we own a business to make money. Making money means you make a profit off of what you sell. But do you know the point at which your business stops spending more money than it takes in and starts generating a profit? That is your break-even point—the point between profit and loss.

Design is a very personal concept. We designers know what it takes to build a design from concept to completion and the steps we take to get there. But frequently we don't know the point at which we are making money. Part of the break-even point is taking into consideration all the elements involved in getting to a cost. Breaking even or even at a loss with your design projects is not always a clear-cut process. Be fair and competitive. In doing so, you create value. When you have value—of your work and time—and you put your best foot forward, you will reach a profit.

Not every job is the same. Part of determining project cost is figuring in your overhead. In a home-based business, utilities, supplies, cell phone, accounting services, transportation, and other expenses all make up your operating costs. Take a few months of projected information and total it up. This will give you a good idea of what it takes to operate per month before any profit is made. Divide by four weeks to determine how much it will take to break even every week. With a home business, it gets tricky to itemize how much electricity, phone, or Internet is devoted solely to your work. A rough estimate gives you at least an idea of what it will cost each month. Your accountant can help you come up with those numbers.

According to the Merriam-Webster dictionary, the break-even point is "the point at which cost and income are equal and there is neither profit nor loss." To get to your break-even point, you need to total your overhead and monthly costs; anything after that should be profit.

If you find that you are not operating in the black, is there something you can live without? Are their expenses you can minimize? Look into your cell phone cost. Maybe there is an option on your phone that you are paying for but not using. Look at your Internet expenses. Is there a less expensive option either with the same company or another company altogether? Can you get your office supplies at another store for a lower price? It's a bit of a juggling act.

I would also seek advice from a bookkeeper or an accountant to help you decipher and understand all the numbers. Graphic design is a subjective type of service. What I think is great design might not be to someone else. One thing that makes it more difficult to examine the break-even point than for other businesses is that every project is totally different. For instance, a tri-fold brochure is a completely different price than a business stationery package. Graphics for the front-end development of a website differ from the design for two retractable banners. So it's hard to pinpoint a black-and-white equation such as, "I will need ten brochures, three retractable banners, and four logo designs to break even." On the other hand, if we had a shoe store, it might be easier to grasp that we need to sell one hundred pairs of shoes to break even.

Clients have to find value in your work. Maintaining top design and business standards is very important in establishing that sense of value. If clients don't know anything about design, they shouldn't do it themselves—in the same way that I wouldn't attempt to renovate my kitchen by myself. I would need to hire a contractor.

Ultimately, what keeps the profits coming is having a steady stream of clients and projects all the time. A break-even point is a constantly moving target, one that will need to be adjusted as you go.

Quotes

As we talk about contracts and quotes, there is an online tool available to streamline that process. It is used by coauthor Jim Smith in his Web design business. I'll let him tell you about it.

QUOTING CLIENTS
by Jim Smith

With every quote I sent out, I used to include a ten-page contract that my attorney helped me create. It covered every possible legal issue but was intimidating to small business clients who, up until that point, had a warm, fuzzy feeling about our business relationship. It took a lot of my time to incorporate the legalese into each quote I gave.

I've since found a much better solution for my business. I use a reasonably priced online application called Quote Roller (quoteroller.com). It is a bit cumbersome to set it up the first time, although it has some nice templates that help quite a bit. But it gives a professional feel to your quotes while making them easy to produce once you have your template ready.

Once your template has been tweaked to your satisfaction, you will just log in, select the option to create a new quote, put in the client's contact info (if they aren't already in the system), add a description of what you will do, select prices from your usual price list, make any changes you want, and send it. A link will be delivered with a nice online version, allowing clients to save and/or print out their own PDF copy. You will get an e-mail when they open it so that you know they have viewed it. They can approve it online with a digital signature, and you will get another e-mail indicating that it has been approved. Or, if you or they prefer to be old-fashioned, they can print a copy, manually sign it, and fax or mail it to you.

Whether you use an online quote builder like Quote Roller or a manually created quote, you can create any sections you want. Mine has these sections:

Introduction

- **Overview:** This is a paragraph defining what the quote is for, with a note that the full description is found under the "Scope of Work" section.

- **About the Company:** Your potential client may or may not know about your company. It is good to include this as part of your boilerplate quote. You can tweak it to personalize it for individual clients if you wish, but it is important to include one to four paragraphs about your company.

Scope of Work

- This is the main part of your quote, where you describe what you are going to do for the client. I include a disclaimer in the scope that states, "Services not listed in this Scope of Work section should be considered additional work and outside of the scope of this proposal."

- If you use a template, you can define your various services, such as brochures, flyers, business cards, logos, etc., under your Scope of Work section. Then it is much easier to simply remove the ones that don't apply to the quote at hand.

Your Role

- I gently remind clients that although I can gladly take care of most of the work, I still need them to provide me with a logo, content, etc. This is where I list exactly what I need them to provide me with and when I need it. Your potential clients will appreciate that you have given them a checklist of what they need to get to you.

Fees

- This is where you can break down the cost of the project. I generally charge a third up front, the second third at the halfway milestone, and the balance when I am ready to turn over the completed work. With Quote Roller, I include a note below the payment table clarifying that the price quoted is the first of three payments. I don't want someone glancing at the cost table and thinking the entire project will cost them a third of what it really does!

Terms and Conditions

- This is the ten pages of legalese provided by my lawyer. It is standard terms that all of my clients must live with, so I make sure it gets into all of my quotes.

To Get Started

- This is very important. Don't just e-mail a quote without indicating what the next step will be. For me, the next step is typically for the client to approve the quote. Then I will generate an invoice to be paid and add the client to my schedule to begin.

Joe America
ABC Manufacturing
123 United Way
Anywhere, CT 00000

Hunter John Designs, llc

Lisa M. Polce
60 Hyde Road
West Hartford, CT 06117
T: 860-841-8517
E: lisa.polce@comcast.net
hjgraphicdesigns.com

06/24/2013

PROJECT TITLE: Design and lay out color retractable banner, 33.5 x 78, with bleeds

Description	Hours	Cost	Total
Design and lay out color retractable banner, 33.5 x 78, with bleeds; client to supply any text, photos, and appropriate logos			
Client revisions			
Prepare files for commercial printing			
Flat fee			$225.00
		Quote	$225.00

Thank you for the opportunity to guide you in the right creative direction.

Nonrefundable deposit of $100 to start project. *Price does not include CT sales tax. Price does not include printing.*

Please make check payable to Hunter John Designs, LLC.

Sincerely yours,

Lisa M. Polce

Lisa M. Polce

Contracts

While we are talking about price, there is one important task ahead of you: You need a contract for your services. When I first started, I trusted everyone. I would even start projects without any money up front. I worked on proofs, through revisions, and even bought stock photography before any money was exchanged. I even released final approved files to printers, which essentially meant my project was complete, except for being paid. Most did pay. It wasn't always in a timely manner, and I even got burned a few times. When I first started, I didn't have enough income to let these clients float by, as most of my own bills had a net of thirty days. It got pretty stressful. I had done my part. These clients had great designs, printed and in use, yet I hadn't received any money.

Believe me, it didn't take too long before I started to get smarter. I started asking for a deposit at the beginning of a project. The amount wasn't very big, but I thought it would be enough of a commitment for the client. Guess what? I got burned again. I finally took the situation seriously and wrote a contract for each design project, explaining different fees and specifying when payment was due. Don't get me wrong—I had taken it seriously before. After all, this was my income. What changed was that I had to stop assuming that everyone was looking out for my own best interests and start treating this as it was and is—a business. I guess that's what is good about writing this book. I can help prevent future home-based business owners from making the same mistakes I did.

I wanted to make it clear in my contract where additional costs or fees could be added so there were no surprises. I made sure there were payments scheduled if the design project involved several components. Because I had been burned in the past, I put in a clause about late fees. If the client is serious about hiring your design firm, then the project should move in a timely manner. I would have clients wait weeks, or even a month, before getting revisions back to my company—and, yes, this was with polite reminders that I needed the revisions back so that the project could progress. I waited and waited. Polite reminders weren't always enough. I would have projects with a turnaround of a few weeks, if that, and some were going on for months. To stop the procrastinators, I made sure to include a late fee in my contract. If the changes and revisions were not back to me within two weeks, there would be a $25 late fee added to the project. Believe me, I don't have projects that drag on anymore. It really worked.

Hunter John Designs, llc

Lisa M. Polce
60 Hyde Road
West Hartford, CT 06117
T: 860-841-8517
E: lisa.polce@comcast.net
hjgraphicdesigns.com

Hunter John Designs, LLC Client Contract

This contract is between Hunter John Designs, LLC and said client, Joe
America, doing business as ABC Manufacturing, Inc. Hunter John Designs, LLC
will have said design projects for ABC Manufacturing, as it pertains to the
business. Our contract proposes that Hunter John Designs, LLC will design a
color retractable banner. The cost of $225 will cover design only. Additional
costs will occur by the following:

- Stock images used **$40 each** (will give said client one **free** stock image).

- Once proof is submitted to client, client has 2 weeks from date submitted to
  have revisions returned to Hunter John Designs, LLC. **Any revisions not
  back in 2 weeks will result in a late fee of $25.** A late fee, thereafter, of
  $10 will occur each time a revision is not back within 2 weeks. In order for
  the project to move smoothly and in a timely manner, Hunter John Designs,
  LLC has to apply this rule. If there are mitigating circumstances that prevent
  the project from finishing in a timely manner, that will be handled on an
  individual basis.

- A nonrefundable deposit will be $100 to begin project.

- Before final files will be released, the remaining balance must be paid with
  additional costs if added, such as CT sales tax, stock images, or late fees.

- All designs are property of Hunter John Designs, LLC. Any reproduction of
  designs or part thereof without proper authorization is strictly prohibited.
  Altering, changing, or selling of designs without proper authorization is
  strictly prohibited.

Hunter John Designs, LLC takes pride in their work. Any project is completed
with teamwork and client input. Hunter John Designs, LLC will keep the client
abreast of any and all progress and have open communication. We look
forward to working with you and thank you for considering Hunter John
Designs, LLC for your design projects. Contact us if you have any questions.
Please sign contract and mail back to us.

Thank you,

Lisa M. Polce   Client Signature_____

Lisa M. Polce

Senior Partner,
Hunter John Designs, LLC

I know this isn't a perfect world. There can be extenuating circumstances that need to be resolved on an individual basis. I speak a lot about the client and your business working as a team. Here's where it counts. People have busy lives. Things can take you off schedule. The best way to handle hiccups in the project is to keep the communication open.

Part of the quote and contract is making sure that everyone is on the same page and the project can move forward. Please have your client sign the contract. If it isn't signed, there is no legal recourse. It needs to be easy to understand and clear so that all involved know what to expect.

Invoices

Jim also uses a nice invoicing service that allows him to streamline that activity. He shares his recommendations for using this service to bill his customers in the sidebar below.

INVOICING CLIENTS
by Jim Smith

In my Web design business, I have found an online tool to streamline my client invoicing task called FreshBooks (freshbooks.com). The program allows me to create a list of clients, send invoices, and give slow payers automatic reminders, and allows clients to pay online. Before I started using it, I was creating invoices through QuickBooks, manually printing them, stamping them, and mailing them. When clients claimed that they had never gotten their invoices, I had to print and mail new copies. When questions arose about an invoice, there was a lot of manual intervention involved. Now, with "cloud" invoicing, I create my weekly invoices and send them out automatically via e-mail. There is a link for my clients to get a PDF version, or they can pay by credit card online. I have a credit card merchant account, but you could set up a PayPal account for less money.

My clients can use that same link to view their accounts, statements, any other outstanding invoices, and payment history. For any clients that insist on using snail mail instead of getting invoices by e-mail, you can even do that

---

Hunter John Designs, llc
Lisa M. Polce
60 Hyde Road
West Hartford, CT 06117
T: 860-841-8517
E: lisa.polce@comcast.net
hjgraphicdesigns.com

Joe America
ABC Manufacturing
123 United Way
Anywhere, CT 00000

07/15/2013

PROJECT TITLE: Design and layout color retractable banner 33.5 x 78, with bleeds
INVOICE NUMBER: 13-027
TERMS: **Due Upon Receipt**

Description	Hours	Cost	Total
Design and layout color retractable banner, 33.5 x 78, with bleeds, client to supply any text, photos and appropriate logos.			
client revisions			
prepare file for commercial printing			
flat fee			$ 225.00
CT sales tax			$ 14.29
		Total	**$ 239.29**

Thank you for the opportunity to guide you in the right creative direction.

Please make check payable to Hunter John Designs, LLC

Sincerely yours,

Lisa M. Polce

Lisa M. Polce

with this service for an added fee. If clients request snail mail, I tell them that the service is available at a $2 surcharge to offset my fee.

You can set terms and automatically assess late fees if you wish. In my own experience when I tried that, it didn't make anyone pay faster; instead, I spent a lot of time rationalizing the extra buck or two while trying to keep the level of hostility down. Now, I still have a late fee clause built into my contracts but never automatically charge it and only use it on rare occasions as leverage for getting a very delinquent payment settled.

One great FreshBooks feature is recurring payments. If I invoice in three monthly payments, for example, I set up a recurring invoice and I set it to go out monthly three times. It sends each invoice automatically, which saves me from so many reminders and the danger of payments slipping through the cracks.

FreshBooks also has features such as multiple languages and currencies. I don't use these, but for those who work with international clients, it is a nice feature. You can also create estimates with this package, if that is useful to you.

Accounting Services

One important aspect of taking care of your money and your business is keeping a good set of books. You have several options available, including the following.

Do-It-Yourself Bookkeeping Services

Many of you will start out this way. With so many software options available, you can pick one and follow the instructions to maintain a good set of books. This is not very complicated as long as your needs are not too complex and you do it faithfully so that you don't get behind. If you have any employees or are involved with a corporation or other businesses, you may want to consider getting some help to make sure everything is done correctly.

Hiring a Bookkeeper

If you started with a do-it-yourself system, you may grow to a point where you aren't inputting your books on a regular basis—or, like many graphic designers, you discover that your time is better spent on getting clients and keeping them happy. Many bookkeepers today prefer to have you scan and e-mail all of your invoices and receipts. As long as you don't mind doing that, it is less expensive than having someone come to you, gather everything together, input it, and generate your reports in your home office.

Hiring a CPA

When I first started my small business, I thought it was important to find a very good CPA (certified public accountant) to handle my books. It cost me a lot of money to have one of his staff come in, gather all my books, take them back to their office, and put them in some semblance of order. Eventually I figured out I was paying my CPA to hire a bookkeeper. That is when I decided I could save a lot of money by hiring my own bookkeeper and just using my CPA for the year-end taxes. You may not even need a CPA for the year-end work, but there are other business ventures involved with my business. If you have your business expenditures providing profits for other business ventures that you own, particularly when some of the businesses involve other individuals, it will give greater credibility to have a CPA's certified opinion on the aspects of your business that impact others. But for your basic set of books for your home-based business, you likely won't need the services of a CPA.

07

Taxes and Record Keeping

Keeping Track of the Money

One of the most important parts of running your business is keeping track of the money. This is important for several reasons:

- Money is the fuel that keeps your business running. Like a gas gauge, you need a money gauge to make sure you don't suddenly run out.
- Money can easily disappear into various projects or expenses without a system for tracking it.
- Money is the unit that bankers, lenders, and others use to measure the health of your business.
- Money is the leveler that the IRS and others use to determine your share of taxes.

My experience is in the United States, but I'm sure this chapter can help you wherever you are. Let's look at some reasons for tracking your money:

- **The fuel:** It can be fun to track your income and profit when things are going well and there is no pressure from a financial slump. But when that slump hits, that is when you really need to track your money. What is causing the slump? Are your sales down? Are you sure? Do you have a system in place to quickly confirm your hunches, or are you going by how you feel?
- **Disappearing money:** I'm not necessarily talking about money disappearing due to theft. If you are the only person with access to the money, you can easily rule that out. But what if you are in a busy time and someone adds a $50 monthly charge to your credit card that you

never approved and don't use? Or what if you are unintentionally providing bigger discounts to favorite customers than you can afford? What if your cell phone contract ran out and the company tripled your rate, hoping you wouldn't notice?

- **Health gauge:** When bankers or lenders start determining if a business is worthy of loans, they don't ask you to write on the application all the reasons you deserve a loan. They don't ask how many free designs you've done for your favorite charity. "Show me the money!" they demand. If you don't have a clear idea of what your business is doing with your money, you won't stand a chance of getting any of their money.

- **Taxes:** Last but certainly not least, you are required by law to track your money so you can share some of it with the various tax agencies. I know you want to stay out of jail for tax fraud or tax evasion, but I also suspect that you are not eager to pay a penny more than you owe the tax man. That means that you will need to keep meticulous, clear records of what you bought for the business and how much income you earned.

Any of those four reasons for tracking your money should convince you of the importance of a good, clean set of books.

What Are You Required to Keep Track Of?

There are some records that you are required by law to keep track of, and there are other records that you don't have to but should. Let's look at the ones you are required to track.

- **Business profit/loss:** The IRS and likely your state or other governing body will require you to declare your quarterly or yearly profit and loss. Not only that, you will also need to break that down into categories of expenses and income depending on the taxable nature of the items. One of the taxes based on your business profit (unless the business is paying tax as a corporation) is self-employment (SE) tax, which covers your Social Security and Medicare taxes.

- **State and municipal sales and use tax:** In Connecticut I must collect sales tax on any work I do, and then I must pay it to the state on a designated schedule. I probably don't need to say this, but this is not my money to do what I want with it until the state asks for it! Put this money in a separate account if you are tempted to use it. The state tax collectors do not tolerate a business owner collecting money for the state and then coming up short when it is time to turn it in. Don't view that money as yours—it isn't! If you are a small business, you may have to pay sales tax to the state. Please seek information pertaining to your specific geographic region and state. Some countries require a VAT (value-added tax). When you are working with tax-exempt businesses such as nonprofits, churches, or synagogues, you will need to have their tax exemption certificate on file. Any type of small business needs to do this. It is complex, so please find out how and where to file your sales tax.

- **Town property tax:** Some towns or localities charge property tax to businesses. When I buy a piece of equipment such as a printer or computer, I add its cost to my list of assets. I must pay property tax on it each year that I have it. There is a declining scale for depreciating the equipment, so by the time it is several years old, I'm only paying property tax on 10 percent of its original value. Make sure when you dispose of an asset to make note of it for next year's evaluation, when you can write it off. I didn't realize I should be doing that, and for a few years I was still paying tax on old printers and laptops I had gotten rid of long ago. Lesson learned. The good news is that my total bill for property tax is less than $20 annually, so it is more of a nuisance tracking the equipment and filing the paperwork than it is coming up with the money each year. But like other taxes, it has to be paid.

- **Employee payroll tax:** If you are planning on bringing in employees, you will have several record-keeping tasks that need to be done. I highly recommend that you get a good payroll company to take care of all the payroll services for you. It doesn't cost much, and these companies are continuously monitoring the payroll laws for your region to keep you out of trouble.

- **Corporate tax:** If you have a taxable corporation, you will be responsible for those taxes as well. Because corporations are beyond the scope of this list, suffice it to say that your accountant will need to set up your record-keeping system properly to be able to generate appropriate records when necessary.

What Else Should You Keep Track Of?

There is a tendency to keep track of your records because you have to. If that is the case, you will only track what is legally required. You will be missing out if you do that. I used to depend on my accountant to give me a bird's-eye view of my business. Was I making a profit? Good. I was working hard, and it was good to know that my business was profitable. Then a slump came, and I felt I was working hard, but the money wasn't coming in. So I'd ask my accountant, "Am I still making a profit?" The response was affirmative. Good. I kept working and not worrying about it.

Over time, I started noticing that my credit cards were maxing out and things didn't feel right. My accountant still reassured me that my business was profitable. Finally I asked the right question and got the answer I needed instead of the accountant's literal answer. "Why is it," I probed, "that I'm working hard trying to replace accounts I've lost, feeling like I'm not paying enough on my loan, juggling my checking account, yet you tell me the business is fine and profitable?" Her answer nearly knocked me off my feet: "The business is profitable, but the reason there isn't enough money to pay some bills is that you keep taking money out for your living expenses." Of course, I took a meager owner's draw every two weeks to pay my mortgage and living expenses. I then learned that an owner's draw (my earnings) does not factor into the profitability of the business. I further learned that to run my business successfully, I needed to get a regular formal report (I call it my quarterly report card), with numbers that I understand and *only* the numbers I needed. If I needed to stop and analyze it, it was not the numbers I wanted. "Make it simple and clear, please" was my new motto.

I got a spreadsheet and created rows for the info I wanted to view on a quarterly basis. Each column is a quarter, so, as time goes on, I can view past quarters and see trends. Here is my report card that I get from my bookkeeper quarterly:

- **Number of clients:** How many clients have used my services in the past quarter? Do I have more or fewer active clients than in past quarters? That is easy to see with this spreadsheet. Perhaps a client is more active than others, but at least I can make sure I'm not relying on one or two clients for all my business.
- **Accounts receivable:** How much money do clients owe me from (1) very recent work, (2) from thirty to ninety days ago, and (3) over ninety days ago? What is the total owed to me for all outstanding invoices? I can tell from

the first row how much money I likely will be getting soon. And from the ninety-plus-day row, I can see if I need to start chasing some slow payers. Most of us have a gut feeling about how much we are owed, but this is a very visual way to get an accurate number.

- **Total sales:** Also known in accounting circles as "accrual sales," this is not the money I've been paid for work I've done last quarter but rather the amount of work I invoiced for. This is an important distinction; it will help you if you can understand the difference between the amount of work you did and the amount you got paid for. I also have rows for some of my bigger accounts, which you may or may not decide to include. It is your report, and you should design it the way you want.
- **Past liabilities:** I have a couple of debts that I have been paying on. I want my report card to show me at a glance what the ending balance is on those. I can make sure quarterly that I'm making headway, and if I'm not, I can start exploring why not.
- **Total expenses:** Like sales, I insist on these numbers being "accrual expenses," or expenses I accrued last quarter rather than expenses I actually paid for. Most of my expenses are relatively insignificant, but if I had utility bills or other expenses, I might break those out to make sure they didn't start increasing.

That's the extent of my report card. It has everything I need. I've documented how each number is formulated so that I don't get accrued sales one quarter and paid sales the next. I've been using this worksheet for over two years now, and it was the best business decision I ever made. My bookkeeper is still not happy with it because it is not structured in accounting terms. In her world, my list of sales and expenses is not the same as hers. But she still produces my report card and, at the same time, produces accounting reports that suit her, my accountant, the tax man, and anyone else who needs to know what my assets and liabilities are. I just want to know how my business is doing!

Who's Responsible for Your Record Keeping?

I used to think record keeping was too complex for us laypersons and should be left to the accountants and bookkeepers. As you might be able to tell from the previous section on keeping track of records, my feelings have changed. When I first started a business, years back, I hired a CPA with a nice, expensive car and a beautiful office. He made all the financial decisions for my business and kept me intimidated enough to allow him to do so. His cost reflected his taste in cars and fancy office decor, so I assumed I shouldn't ask questions and just let him perform his magic.

I finally learned that I was not taking responsibility for my own business and didn't understand enough to make my own decisions. That was not why I got into my own business. I wanted to make my own informed decisions. I wanted to have people like this CPA working for me, helping me learn how to make my own decisions. That is when I did something rash—I fired him. Of course, I didn't do it dramatically. I just told him I didn't need his services, thank you very much.

Then I started being a responsible businessperson. I interviewed some accountants and some attorneys. I preplanned the questions for the interview—questions such as, "What other small businesses do you work with?" and "Why do you think you and I would be a good match?" and "What are your rates for small businesses like mine?" If I felt intimidated by the answer or if I felt I couldn't ask the person tough questions when my business needed help, he or she got crossed off my list of potential team members. What a feeling of power! Finally I was in charge of my business. I needed a team of professionals to help me, but ultimately I wanted people who worked on my team, not ones sitting in a fancy office dictating what I must do to succeed.

I found a CPA I felt very comfortable with, and I use him to this day. He is extremely bright but doesn't put on false airs. My attorney, who is quiet and unassuming, not only has a law degree but is also a CPA. Do I need all that brainpower for my small business? Probably not. But he is also a very good listener and a wise sage I can rely on to give me sound advice when I'm not looking at the entire picture. And both of these team members respect the fact that I'm a small business owner who doesn't have big corporate pockets that they can use to build up their retirement fund. Rates are reasonable, quick advice is free, and they are truly team members. And I get to be responsible for my own business.

So if you have found someone else to be responsible for your record keeping or your legal matters, find out if that person is confident enough to let you become responsible for your own actions. If so, welcome him or her onto your team; if not, fire that person and start interviewing for a replacement.

(Note: Information in this chapter was gathered from interviews with F. William O'Connor, Esq., and David Ryan Polgar, Esq., specializing in entertainment and copyright law.)

Owning your own business means facing legal and ethical issues. You sure don't want any legal issues, and you want to be protected. I highly recommend hiring an attorney for setting up your business, contracts, subcontractors, non-compete clauses, nondisclosure clauses, etc. You don't want to be caught off guard. Remember, the nice guys in business can get hurt.

The legal and ethical advice in this chapter is strictly for informational purposes and general advice. This chapter will also discuss, in general, copyright issues as they pertain to your projects and clients' work. Please seek an attorney for any legal or ethical issues as they pertain to your state and business. I live and do business in Connecticut, and laws differ by region and circumstances.

When Do You Need an Attorney?

Small business owners hesitate to turn to an attorney because they either feel like it's not necessary or fear that it will be too expensive. I suggest that you contact an attorney or accountant, even if it is just for a consultation. There is nothing wrong with understanding the material enough to do it yourself, but I wouldn't recommend it. It's like when you know someone who tried to do graphic design by himself, and when you looked at his work, it wasn't very good. The same logic should apply to legal issues in your business. Usually, when you try to do something yourself to save money, it costs you much more in the long run than it would have if you had sought outside help in the first place. Once you are in hot water legally, it will get expensive to iron it out.

You should use an attorney for basic guidance and general direction for the small business owner. The nature of your business dictates how much legal advice you need. If you own a graphic design business, make sure to take the necessary precautions.

Sole Proprietorship, Partnership, LLC, or Corporation?

There are several ways to set up your business, such as sole proprietorship, limited liability corporation (LLC), and partnership. There are also corporations, but for most readers of this book, corporations are probably overkill.

Sole Proprietorship

This is also known as "Doing Business As" (DBA). The benefit is that it's relatively easy and inexpensive to set up your business as sole proprietor. The problem is that the exposure to potential legal action is huge. People can come after your personal assets via lawsuits. These personal assets can include your bank accounts, house, stocks and investments, and college savings. Although your graphic design business isn't a likely target for a lawsuit, remember that you will have no protection of your personal assets if you choose to be a sole proprietor. That's pretty scary. It might be less expensive to set up a sole proprietorship, but the exposure to you, a small business owner, may not be worth the risk.

There are other things you need to worry about if you choose to do it yourself without getting a lawyer involved. You will likely have to register with the Department of Labor and the Internal Revenue Service (IRS) in the United States. At the state level, you will probably find a mound of paperwork to deal with; many states do not seem "small business friendly."

Partnership

Another kind of business you can have is a partnership. In a partnership, two or more individuals enter a formal agreement to own the business together. There are two main types of partnerships: general partnership and limited partnership. A general partnership is what you would think of for a partnership—two or more people in business together. A limited partnership has one or more general partners (frequently thought of as working partners) plus one or more limited partners, or partners who have no management authority (frequently thought of as silent partners) whose liability is restricted to the amount of his or her investment. Neither is seen very often. A partnership can get complicated because state and local laws vary. It can also expose you to liability.

Limited Liability Corporation (LLC)

I do not recommend trying this approach by yourself. When I was interested in actually naming my business and getting an LLC, I tried to go it alone. I figured I would research how to set up an LLC on the Internet and start filling out the paperwork. I used the state's website, kept clicking through links, and even found where I could begin filling in the information. I felt like I went through so many links that I didn't even know if I was on the same website anymore. I got really frustrated with that. I found the state's site confusing (imagine that!) and not very user-friendly.

I am old-fashioned when it comes to putting my information out on the Internet. Because I was clicking through so many pages, I wasn't about to enter personal information on a page when I wasn't sure where the information was going. In addition to that, there were questions to which I didn't know the answer because I wasn't sure what they were asking. So trying to do it myself came to a quick end. When I started my LLC, I turned to an attorney to handle the setup of the business. It was worth it to me to have it done right, and have it done right the first time.

All states have LLCs. They are inexpensive, easy, flexible, and a much less formal type of ownership than a full corporation. You need to elect how to tax your income, and it's completely up to you as long as you are reporting your income. I use a Schedule C. The limited liability corporation is intended to do exactly what it says: limit your liability. In other words, if you are being sued, the person cannot come after your personal assets. Moreover, some businesses that hire you will want you to have an LLC. This gives you legitimacy and credibility, and it should certainly make you feel better as a small business owner to have it.

If you want to obtain an LLC, it is to your advantage to do so under legal guidance. An attorney takes care of all the paperwork and explains how it pertains to your particular state and business. If the state says you are a limited liability entity, people will know you are protected. You will also be assigned an Employer Identification Number (EIN).

One piece of advice to walk away with: If you are an LLC, make sure you use the identity all the time—every time you sign something, in all your print materials, on business stationery, and on your website. As the owner, if you sign anything under the LLC umbrella, you are considered a member (e.g., Lisa Polce, member, Hunter John Designs, LLC).

If you don't take your LLC seriously, individuals and companies can find ways to go after your assets if something goes wrong. So take it seriously and always use the proper wording. You are running a business. If you don't use the LLC on all your paperwork, or if you use it inconsistently, you can get in trouble. If you have documents, especially contracts with clients, where you are not using your LLC, the courts will assume that you didn't really care you were running an LLC business and find you personally responsible for whatever went wrong. You may still need to go to court someday, but you will be prepared to defend your business as a formal LLC.

Another piece of advice: You must keep your business and personal finances separate. If there are problems down the road and you haven't kept things separate, the court system can come after your personal assets.

Corporations

Single member or multi-member corporations benefit from a strong body of corporate law. You need to have a good understanding of case statutes that protect you. There are specific rules you need to respect and be diligent about following. C corporations are much more formal, requiring such tasks as annual meetings, corporate filings with your state, annual reports, and even more government reports. You will also need a board of directors. Corporations are subject to double taxation (i.e., corporate earnings taxes). Owners pay a tax on distribution and double taxation on dividends. Some corporations use stock.

Corporations have many requirements. Subchapter S, or S corporations, offer many benefits while protecting you from being subject to double taxation. If you are considering an S corporation, make sure your attorney explains the difference between that and a limited liability corporation.

Legalities of Contracts

A contract allows you to be clear about what you are being paid to do and the service you are providing. I have mentioned this before, but I'll mention it again: Do not do business without quotes and/or contracts. It will only come back to haunt you if you don't protect yourself at the beginning. No matter how nice the person seems or how well you know him or her, it's still business. Treat the transaction as such.

Bill O'Connor, a small business attorney in Avon, Connecticut, says, "You are running a business, so act like it. Having a contract avoids the 'he said, she said' issues. Any verbal agreements don't apply."

There are programs and applications you can buy so that you have templates for contracts. You can make your own, or your local office supply store likely carries blank contract forms. As I have said before, if you choose to do your contracts yourself, please at least pay a lawyer review them and even offer advice on how to individualize them for your business and guidelines.

The contract protects you in many aspects. When you do it yourself, things might go as expected. It is when something goes wrong that you realize your do-it-yourself contract has loopholes or wording that won't hold up in court. You want to limit your liability to your business. The consequences when something goes wrong with you or your client can be serious. Arbitration can be expensive, and you don't want the formality of court proceedings. Contracts can protect you and ensure that you continue to get paid. And your mission as a business owner is always to get paid.

Nondisclosure and Non-compete Clauses

Nondisclosure and non-compete clauses are essential for business owners. It's another way of protecting you and your business.

A nondisclosure agreement protects any information an employee has access to that is kept confidential and proprietary. Here again, make sure you understand what you are signing.

Non-compete clauses are basically protection from someone stealing your ideas or clients away from your business. If you hire people, even just as independent contractors, they can "steal" your clients. If they form close enough relationships with your clients to do business with them, the non-compete clause protects you. There is usually a "time and distance" stipulation; in other words, once an employee no longer works for you, he or she can't operate within a certain amount of time or distance from your place of business. The time clause usually specifies the amount of time they must wait before contacting any of your clients. (Most agreements state a year to two years.) Distance must also be reasonable. For instance, a clause might state that any independent contractor or employee of mine can't operate a similar business in my state of Connecticut for a year. That would be a pretty unreasonable stipulation, and the contractor or employee would most likely fight it in court. A more reasonable agreement might be within a twenty-mile radius of your location.

Again, please seek an attorney's advice for these types of contracts with your employees or independent contractors. These clauses are also easy to set up before you "hire" someone. It's more difficult to implement one after you have hired employees, so do it before they start working.

Subcontractors and Independent Contractors

Subcontractors and independent contractors are people you hire but don't take on as official employees of your business. It seems like an easy way out of being so formal about an employee. This not a black-and-white area, however, and should be treated with the seriousness that it deserves. It is very difficult to be an independent contractor. If something goes wrong, it is almost never agreed on that this person was an independent contractor. There is a twenty-question checklist in the state of Connecticut to prove that an employee was indeed an independent contractor.

When employees are getting paid and working on a controlled schedule, they are considered typical employees. If they are working for several people, have their own schedule, and set their own hours, then they are likely independent contractors. If you are in this situation, please seek legal advice and have the proper paperwork drawn up to protect yourself. If the person in question is proven to have been an employee and not an independent contractor, you can be liable for back taxes, FICA, Social Security, workmen's compensation, and other fees that come with having staff. If you have just one employee on your payroll, you will also need an employee handbook.

Be careful when someone asks you to recommend a professional in a related industry. For example, if someone approaches me to recommend a photographer, I try to give that person two or three colleagues' names. It's best to recommend more than one. If for some reason it doesn't work out and you only recommended one person, the ill-fated recommendation usually comes back to bite you. Another way to protect yourself is to get out there in your industry and related fields and get to know other professionals. If possible, hire them yourself so you can gain a better understanding of how they operate and handle you as a client. It's a pretty good bet that if they have handled you well, they will do the same with people you refer to them.

This information provides just a snapshot of what you need to think about when starting your own business. Don't be penny wise and pound foolish, as the old saying goes. You really need to seek legal and accountant services. It is better to pay someone for professional services now to protect yourself in the future. If you don't understand something, ask. You likely don't know the law or accounting procedures well enough to navigate them on your own, and ignorance is not protection from the law.

Copyright Issues

The American Institute of Graphic Arts (AIGA) website (aiga.org/copyright-basics-for-graphic-designers) states:

> Copyright is the exclusive right to control reproduction and commercial exploitation of your creative work. Copyright protects any kind of artwork, including illustrations, photographs and graphic design. Except under certain circumstances . . . you own the copyright in your work at the moment you create it in a "fixed" form of "expression." A fixed form of expression is any tangible medium that can be perceived by humans, including traditional forms—such as paintings, sculptures, writings—and new forms that require a machine to perceive (e.g., GIF files, CDs, websites).

I know that sounds really formal, with many facets to understand. You can get more information from the US Copyright Office or AIGA, a great organization with local chapters throughout the US. AIGA has a wealth of information on its website and helps you meet colleagues in your industry.

As a graphic designer, you will likely create original work. You can license various photos or images, or you can use public domain images or art that might come with the graphic applications that you buy. Public domain means just that: The public can use the images at any time, and the public can use the same exact image you might be using—and you can't do anything about it. It is better to use various stock image sites or create original work.

Copyright is part of our history. It is protected by the US Constitution. It was created to help promote creativity, to prevent our arts and sciences from becoming stale, and to protect the original authorship of designers and artists. The US Copyright Office has a wealth of information to help you understand the intricacies of copyright.

Copyright is in the US Constitution (Article I, Section 8, Clause 8), which states, "The Congress shall have the power . . . to promote the Progress of Science and useful Arts, by securing for limited Times to Authors and Inventors the exclusive Right to their respective Writings and Discoveries."

As David Polgar explains, "In other words, it is a limited monopoly by the author for the purpose of incentivizing creative works. You do not need to register your copyright. You have the copyright as soon as you create your work. You can take the next best step by registering your copyright with the Library of Congress, and you can even do this online. It also is a good idea to use the copyright symbol with your work, like this: ©."

Everything has terms and conditions. Make sure you read them. I know it sounds tedious, but you need to know what you are using and what rights you have to use it. A stock photography site, where you purchase an image to use in your design, is called a clearinghouse. With an online photo company like iStockPhoto.com, you are buying the right to use the photo, not the photo itself. There are sites that offer a blanket license. Normally, the price will be more per photo for blanket licenses. Having a license means you have Creative Commons, which is typically less expensive than actually owning the copyright. You don't have a lot of control over it. For instance, if you write a play and don't care if someone uses it, you will just want some type of credit that it's your play.

Technology continues to move at lightning speed, giving us more instant access to information and creativity. With the instant access, such as via the Internet, it is easy to overstep your bounds with copyright use. Even as graphic design has developed, we still need to keep the basics in mind when it comes to creating original marketing materials. David Polgar says, "Technology moves so much faster than law, and we are currently in the game of catch-up."

With technology moving so fast, there is so much out there that makes it easier and easier to obtain information or images, but we have to be careful how we use them.

Utilizing Photos

Don't use Google to search for images as a source of photos. Most Google photographs are copyrighted in some way, and using them in your design work without obtaining the proper permission is breaking copyright law. There have been court cases where professionals have gotten away with "work" they found on the Internet, but that doesn't make it the norm. A client of mine paid a photo company a large sum to settle a case in which an employee used a couple of photos from the Internet for its website. It is not a recommended method of getting photos. Amateur and professional photographers will license their photos at a much cheaper rate than commercial websites, and they can be much more cost-effective for your client and project.

When using your own photography, make sure that anyone who appears in the photo signs a photo release form. You need their permission to use a photo that has them in it. The general rule of thumb is that if they can be recognized, you need their permission. If it's a sweeping shot or an overview of a crowded street, you probably don't need release forms. Be cautious with your own photography.

Fair Use

Fair use is a First Amendment right that allows an individual a certain level of flexibility when using someone else's material without permission. Fair use balances several factors, such as criticism, comments, news reporting, teaching, or research. It really depends on how much of the copyrighted material you use. As stated by Dave Polgar, "Fair use is a shield, not a sword. It's a defense."

For example, if you use a line from a song, that may be okay. If you are using the whole song in a video and post that video, that's a violation of fair use laws. Fair use is a Rubik's Cube that depends on the purpose and nature of the material, how much you are using, and if you are hindering the rights holder's ability to profit from it. For example, if you quote forty-four lines out of ten thousand, it could be considered fair use. If you quote forty-four lines of a sixty-line poem, it could be violating copyright laws. This is just a simplified anecdotal example. Be sure you do your own research and seek legal advice from professionals before using copyrighted material such as song lyrics.

According to Polgar, fair use is a balancing act of the following factors:

- Reason for using material and its purpose (educational versus entertainment)
- Nature and reason of the copyrighted material being used (factual versus creative)
- Amount and length of material copied, depending on how large a portion you use
- Effect on the market (lost revenue or sales due to using material without permission)

The safest way to protect yourself is to ask permission of the copyright owner. And get it in writing so you have proof of the granted permission.

Polgar also mentions public domain. Public domain material can be freely used by writers and filmmakers without permission. Material can be in the public domain because the copyright protection has expired or the creator has decided to make the content available.

Some clip art that comes on your computer or in Microsoft Office is public domain. If you use artwork through online services such as Vistaprint, the images on their website are public domain. In other words, anyone can use those images, and you can be using artwork that other businesses use. Therefore, you are not setting yourself apart from others. I see this often when people try to do it themselves. I can spot an order from Vistaprint very easily.

Copyright is in the US Constitution to promote the arts and sciences and maximize the level of creativity. Graphic designers need to stay up to date with US copyright laws and even consult with an entertainment and copyright attorney if necessary. You own the copyright to your work as soon as you write it down. Registering that work with the Library of Congress protects it even more.

Work for Hire

The following information was adapted from "Copyright Ownership and Transfers FAQs" by Rich Stim of the Stanford Copyright and Fair Use Center (fairuse.stanford.edu/overview/copyright-research/ownership-and-transfers). This link provides explanations of some terms frequently used to describe copyright issues. Graphic designers deal mostly with "work for hire" projects. When we have a contract to do a brochure, for instance, the work will be work for hire. In the end, the client owns the copyright for what you produce. If I wanted to show a PDF of a brochure design I did for a client in this book, for instance, I would have to go to the client and ask for permission to use it. Usually the person who creates a work is also the owner of the copyright, but because you were paid to design the brochure, the person who paid you owns the work at the end of the project.

In many circumstances, a person who pays someone else to create a work becomes the initial copyright owner, not the person who actually created it. The resulting works are called "works made for hire" (or sometimes simply "works for hire").

According to Stim, the following types of work qualify as work for hire:

- a work created by an employee within the scope of employment, or
- a commissioned work that falls within a certain category of works and that is the subject of a written agreement.

If the work qualifies under one of these two methods, the person paying for the work (the hiring party) is the author and copyright owner. If you want to use the work, you should seek permission from the employer or hiring party, not the person who created the work.

One question that comes up often: Is there a difference between an author and a copyright owner? The author is the first owner of a copyright. He is either the creator of the work or the person who employs someone to create the work. Many authors do not retain their copyright ownership; they sell or transfer it to someone else in return for a lump sum payment or periodic payments known as royalties.

"Work for hire" transfers copyright from the actual creator to the person who hires the creator. This is particularly important for graphic designers; you do not want to be accused of copyright infringement. There is a fine line when it comes to designing and copyright concerns. As a designer, this is where your ethics should come in. If you use another person's work in your design, you need to get permission and give that designer credit. If you hire a photographer and use his or her photos, you will need permission to use them. That can be done with a simple photo credit line in your project.

Dave Polgar suggests that just because something is legal doesn't mean you'll do it, and just because something is illegal doesn't mean you won't do it. Copyright law is an *extremely* gray area that is constantly evolving. Knowing the right questions to ask puts you in a good position. Please consult a copyright lawyer for more information. Be honest with yourself and your clients' projects. Make sure your design work is authentic and different. It's not worth the risk of being sued for copyright infringement. For more detailed information on copyright issues, refer to *The Copyright Handbook* by Stephen Fishman.

The graphic design industry lends itself to being, for lack of a better word, creative. Clients hire you based on your experience, your portfolio, and the integrity you bring to the project. They come to you for your expertise in your field and the skills you offer. Always strive to do your best and be original. Your customers are counting on you to create something that will make them stand out above their competition. You as a professional will also stand out with your design. It is a constant challenge to be better than before. How can I make this the best brochure or the most unique logo so that my client has effective marketing materials? We put a lot of pressure on ourselves to exceed our clients' expectations, as well as our own.

When you feel strongly about a design after your work is completed, be sure to review with your client what is protected. After all, it's your work. Be proactive and, whenever possible, seek advice from legal professionals. Remember, there are standards we must meet within the industry to maintain integrity and professionalism. You are a reflection of this industry, and so is your work. Be proud of it, and be proud to adhere to the copyright laws that are there to protect our designs.

Marketing Your Business

Marketing is one of those things that business owners sometimes don't take seriously enough. You have your office set up. You have your LLC, sole proprietorship, or corporation established. You have business cards. So how do you market yourself, your business, your skills, your expertise, and your edge over the competition to gain clients and continued success? Remember, having a client buy your services means you are generating income.

When I finally decided to name my business and get an LLC so that I felt like I had officially arrived as a business owner, my next step was to get out there and market my company. Once I had my paperwork done and could officially say, "I own my own business," I needed to get out and start meeting people, networking, and exposing my business. I don't tend to think big, but I wanted to be a household name, at least in my community. Nothing like setting a challenge for myself.

What I'm trying to tell you is that business doesn't come to your door; you have to get out there and look for it. I've mentioned this a few times, but it bears repeating: Owning a business is not for people who consider themselves shy. If you are shy, I highly recommend taking public speaking classes or some type of Dale Carnegie course.

Public Relations

As you grow your business and wade in the waters of success, don't ever be afraid to toot your own horn. Part of owning your own business is wearing your public relations hat. Public relations is an integral part of making yourself and your business look good, in theory, without buying advertising space. Public relations is, in part, making your business look good in the eyes of your audience.

If you know any public relations professionals in your area, contact them and get their professional opinion. Ask them questions or even hire them to help you attract attention to your business. I had a head start on this front because I had a BA in communications, with concentrations in advertising and public relations. I am by no means saying that I know everything, nor do my suggestions qualify as professional public relations advice. These are just the tips I have learned through my education and the experiences I have had during my career.

You can use various media outlets and local papers to bring attention to your business. Noteworthy occasions include, but are not limited to, adding an employee, winning an industry-related award, gaining certification, donating to a local cause, or participating in a fund-raiser. Speaking at local community events and at other engagements also brings positive attention to your business. Just as writing your résumé seems like an overwhelming task, so does making yourself look good. Business owners need to gain exposure by letting the general public know what they are doing as it pertains to running their businesses. The most important thing, of course, is to do so in a professional manner.

Most people think of public relations, or what they often call "crisis relations," only when things go badly. Examples of crisis relations would be ExxonMobil after the Exxon Valdez oil spill or BP after the spill in the Gulf of Mexico. These companies spent many years repairing their reputations after the disasters.

We all need public relations when things go drastically wrong, but it's just as important to do it when we have good things to report. It's hard to pat yourself on the back as a business owner and bring attention to yourself. But you are all you've got to make this business successful. If you win an award, complete a course, donate to an organization, or help at a fund-raiser, these all warrant drawing attention to your business.

Press Releases

You can start your public relations efforts with a general press release, which is typically sent to local media outlets. These outlets can include newspapers, magazines, and television stations. The press release gives an overview of what you are trying to bring attention to so that they can write a story about you or, at the very least, include some type of mention in a local town news section.

The press release should include:

- **Headline:** What is your key point? Get the readers' attention so that they want to read more.

- **Body copy:** Be careful when grabbing the media's attention, because they likely don't have time to research your text. The journalist will take information directly from your press release, so be sure to be accurate. As in your graphic designs, make it easy for the journalist to read the release. You don't want it to be complicated. Make sure you generate interest in the first few sentences. If they are like any other journalist, they are on crazy deadlines and want quick, easy-to-read information.

- **The five Ws:** Just as I do when designing for a client, I first try to think of the five Ws—who, what, where, when, why—and, most likely, how. These should all be covered in the message. The message has to be clear, consistent, and accurate. Even when announcing an event, keep in mind the Ws. If you fill in the basics, the information will be clear to the reader. Remember when you're writing a press release that you want to draw attention to your company. Make sure your company is worthy of that attention and that you are not wasting anyone's time.

- **Information about your company:** Again, make it short and sweet. Describe your company and what it's all about. Most information can be found in your printed materials, such as in your brochures, or on your website. Always include some way to contact you or direct the journalist to your website. Spell out the whole URL to avoid confusion.

- **Contact information:** Include the name of your company and your full name, address, city, state, phone number, and e-mail.

For Immediate Release
Hunter John Designs, LLC, Announces Launch of New Website
West Hartford, CT—July 19, 2013

Hunter John Designs, LLC, a graphic design firm serving the greater Hartford area, launched a new website.

As fast as technology advances, you need to stay fresh with your business. This local graphic design firm sizzles with its new website. You need to get visitors to do one important task when they visit your website: contact you. This new website grabs the visitors' attention. Hunter John Designs, LLC, owner Lisa Polce states, "We wanted to give new life to a great marketing tool. It's exciting to see the traffic increase and instantly have new, unique visitors when you just do something as simple as changing it up."

There are so many reasons to have a website. Just make sure it's the right reason for your business.

The Internet is filled with potential customers. Any business needs to stay on top of its game. Without a design that catches the eye and, more importantly, gives potential clients a great first impression of your business, you will sink to the bottom of the search list.

Hunter John Designs, LLC, has been privately owned for five years. The company prides itself on having exceptional customer service and delivering a great first impression with a company's marketing materials. Great first impressions get the next customer or client to contact you. Hunter John Designs, LLC, continues to surpass its goals and is gaining ground in the advertising and marketing industry.

Polce stays active in many organizations, including the Advertising Club of Connecticut and West Hartford Chamber of Commerce and a local Business Network International (BNI) chapter.

For more information or to inquire, you may contact Lisa Polce at (860) 841-8517 or lisa.polce@comcast.net. Visit her website at hjgraphicdesigns.com.

Networking to Market Your Business

Sounds so simple, doesn't it? Get out and network. Networking is work—hard work. After all, the word is net*work*, not net-lazy, not net-easy, and not net-if-I-feel-like-it. Networking is a two-way street that starts with you, but if you think it's *all* about you, you are wrong. Networking is truly wanting the other person to be successful with the hope that any success comes back to you.

Traditional ad space is expensive. Business networking is less expensive, if not free in some cases, and it's more personal. It involves more than just passing out business cards, though. To get the most out of trying to market my business, I started attending various networking meetings. I actually don't ask for a business card until I have spoken with the person. If all you are after is how many business cards you can collect at the end of the night, your networking and business will suffer.

You will hear a lot that networking is building relationships. You need to get to know people before you can do business with them or, even better, refer them. You will also have to like crowds and be able to interact with different groups of people.

You don't have to be in a meeting to think about giving business to someone you know. I have trained my ears to listen to what's going on around me. It can be something as simple as standing in line at a grocery store and striking up a conversation with the person in front of me. You never know where that conversation might take you.

A NETWORKING SUCCESS STORY

About a year ago, I met a holistic health coach who had just relocated from Danbury, Connecticut, to West Hartford at a networking event. I made sure I introduced myself to her, as I felt I had many connections that could help her. Also, as a member of a BNI chapter, the West Hartford Chamber of Commerce, and the Advertising Club of Connecticut, I brought her around with me to introduce her to my business contacts at various meetings. Several months went by, and we would catch up at different meetings and frequently meet for coffee.

As time went on, not only did we become colleagues, we also became good friends. When she was ready, she hired my company to do her logo, business card, rack card, and a vinyl banner. When she decided to move forward with her branding package, she said to me, "I want to work with you because you are sincere, talented, and I see you in action. You are so willing to help others. I really admire that in you, so I want to hire you for my branding package."

I was honored to have her as my client. And, let me tell you, those kind words meant a lot to me. Remember, networking is about helping someone first; then that help comes back to you. It's about building relationships.

In the years since I started as a business owner, the way I network has changed dramatically. Networking is something you continually work at to hone your listening, speaking, and sales skills. I used to be the kind of person who stood back and observed. My very first lesson in coming out of my shell came when I decided to go back to school at the age of twenty-six to finish my degree. I had only a few college credits, so you could say I was starting over. I won't bore you with the details, but I moved away to go to college and attended Jacksonville University in Jacksonville, Florida.

When I drove onto the campus for the first time, I didn't know a soul. As I unpacked my car and made the trips up and down the stairs from the car to my room, I realized that if I didn't speak up and introduce myself, it was going to be a lonely first few days or even weeks. It wasn't easy, but I had to break that "step back and observe" habit and speak up, introduce myself, make eye contact, and make myself likable. The whole experience was daunting, but I look back on going back to school away from home, outside my comfort zone, as the best thing I ever did.

My first friend was Danielle, and we are still close friends twenty years later. I happened to be walking by, and she was trying to get into her dorm with her hands full. I stopped and asked if I could help her, and our friendship grew from there. I mention this story because it's a lot like networking. You have to be willing to speak up and introduce yourself, but most importantly, you have to think about how you can help the person in front of you.

The Farming vs. Hunting Approach

Networking is a like planting a seed. You can think of the two main approaches as hunting versus farming. In farming, a seed takes time to grow. That time in networking involves getting to know someone and investing in their business relationship. Make time to meet the person for coffee or have a one-on-one meeting to get to know each other better. Building that relationship will likely lead to someone giving you a referral.

"Hunting" is more of a selfish approach to networking—in theory a one-way street. It asks, "What's in it for me? What can I get out of this person?" I often tell people that if they are in the graphic design business for themselves alone, then they should pack their bags. They won't succeed. Just like in any other relationship, your business relationships need to be a two-way street. It's important to help someone before you help yourself. It's a powerful way of thinking. You get business by giving business.

If you're only in it for yourself, people will pick up on it. Networking is about connecting to others. How many people do you know who can help someone else you know, not just by possibly doing business with them, but because their areas of expertise complement one another? You come with your own Rolodex. Maybe the person you are talking to needs the expertise of someone else you know. By conveying that information and making that connection, you have planted the seed of who you are in that person's mind. If you are "hunting," you are in people's faces and being obnoxious. Think about the last time you were networking. Were you acting like an annoying, pushy salesperson? If so, that's a good way to push people away from you.

It's hard starting out. I know that. You want that money coming in, but the biggest turnoff to fellow networkers is sounding desperate. As the saying goes, "You can spend a lot of time getting customers, but you can lose them in a second." Take the time to do it right. The more you network, the more your business will grow and the better you will get at it. People tend to want lasting relationships. Surround yourself with people who are authentic and who deliver on their business promises.

Face-to-Face Networking in a Digital World

As much as technology evolves, allowing us to make instant connections in the digital world, it still doesn't replace face-to-face interaction. Sure, an e-mail, tweet, text, or instant message comes in handy, but there is weight in the old-fashioned handshake, eye contact, and making a good introduction.

The digital world puts a net over us sometimes. You have a client across the country, but you must capitalize on human interaction as well and keep polishing the art of networking. The better someone knows you, the more business that person will do with you. It is as simple as that.

I am an old-fashioned business owner. I don't forget where I came from. I don't forget my first couple of years of self-employment. I have been there, done that. It makes me feel good to share my experiences and my stories to help the next person trying to start his or her own business. It doesn't have to be a graphic design business; the sincerity is still there. You can certainly discover your own style, your own introduction, your own way of doing things, but you will always go far remembering that you were once where they are. The more you help someone else, the more that same kindness comes back to you. As they say, what goes around comes around.

Networking Organizations

When you join any organization, you can't just be a member and have a certificate on your wall. You have to be an *active* member. If you join something, say you are a member, and then never participate or commit yourself to being involved, you will never get your money's worth out of the organization. Most likely, you will not renew. Whether it is a chamber, networking group, industry-related organization, or a monthly business meeting, you have to be involved, committed, and loyal to the organization. Take on some type of involvement like joining a committee or assuming a leadership role.

You might also volunteer your time or speak at different functions when the topic is relevant to your business. You can gain valuable exposure that way. Speaking at functions will add credibility to your career and validate your industry knowledge. Again, the certificate on the wall won't get you new business or clients; your involvement with and dedication to networking organizations gets you exposure and new business.

You should visit various networking meetings and see what's a good fit for you and your business. It can get expensive having to pay fees for the different meetings, so you don't have to join a lot of them all at once. Research area networking meetings or look on your town website. Talk to your colleagues to see what they attend, and don't be afraid to ask if you can go as a guest. I am flattered and honored to bring colleagues as my guests. It is not a bother; I am glad to share my experiences and introduce people to potential business contacts.

Some organizations have member profiles on their websites. That's another way to be out there in front of the public for free. Ultimately, being involved with these organizations is free advertising for your home-based business.

Business Network International (BNI)

Business Network International (BNI) was founded by Dr. Ivan Misner. BNI has local chapters all over the world, so there is bound to be a chapter near you. As stated on the BNI website, "The philosophy of this organization is built on the idea of Giver's Gain: By giving business to others, you will get business in return. This is predicated on the age-old idea of 'what comes around goes around.'"

I have been a BNI member since 2009. Our local chapter is thirty members strong. We are a professional referral group. One of the advantages of BNI is that each chapter has one seat per represented profession. I'm the only graphic designer in my group; no other graphic designer can join.

BNI is a great way to get business. It's a structured meeting that usually happens early in the morning. In the corporate world, we all have had that one meeting we had to go to each week. Well, this is my once-a-week sales meeting. My chapter has a great mix of personalities, professions, and friendships that make it fun. All chapters have their own way of doing things, different personalities, and other related industries that might make one better to join than another.

In my experience, BNI has been great. As with anything you join, you must maintain a certain level of commitment, engagement, and loyalty. I have thirty members who are basically my sales team. As these people go about their week, they are listening for people who might need graphic design services. Now, do I come to the meeting with a referral and do I leave with a referral every week? No, but being a BNI member and a part of this organization has certainly gotten me business and has given my business great exposure. I, in return, have given referrals to members of the group, and they have received business from me.

I encourage you to visit various chapters in your area and see if it is a good fit for you. Visit the national website at BNI.com. Ask your colleagues if they are members of BNI and, if so, what their experience has been with their chapter. In my chapter, we have people who have been members for over five years. That is great loyalty. Once you have visited a couple of chapters, decide if it's your style with its represented professions, structure, and personalities. BNI isn't for everyone. If it's for you, you will have good return on investment (ROI).

With BNI, business will come to you as you gain the members' trust and build your reputation. You have a captive audience. You are giving an introduction to your business every week. The business ball starts rolling when the members hire you to design their marketing materials. As you do business with the members, the members begin to trust you and talk about you with other BNI members and their colleagues.

Part of a BNI meeting involves testimonials. Once you do business with a member, that member gives you a testimonial in front of the whole chapter. Testimonials help other members decide if they want to do business with you. Just as in any business transaction with a new client, create an experience and style of business that people want to talk about. If you treat people how you want to be treated, it eventually comes back to you. The ball keeps rolling. Once a member gives you a testimonial, it gives other members an incentive to hire you or refer your business.

Networking is a seed you need to plant in order to grow a level of respect in the business world. By networking and getting out there to do as much as you can to nurture that seedling, your business grows. As you can see, networking is hard work.

Introducing Your Business

Because networking is constantly changing, I am always working on my introduction to make it sizzle. An introduction is a thirty-second speech to explain what you do for a living—that all-important "elevator speech." You want the person to ask for more information or be intrigued enough to want to speak with you after the meeting.

Working on your introduction is a constant process. I try not to let it get too stale by saying the same thing every time. What should your introduction include? In a few short sentences, maybe thirty seconds, tell me what you do so that it piques my interest to learn more. Once you have a person's attention, there is certainly time after the meeting to elaborate on what you have to offer. As for your introduction in a networking meeting, tell your audience what you do and what problem you solve for clients. Why would someone want to hire you or refer you? Create a reason for someone to want to know more about you.

SAMPLE INTRODUCTION 1

Good morning. I'm here to help you look good. Did you come to this meeting wanting to give a great first impression? Well, that's what I do with my clients. I give them a great first impression with their marketing materials. You have to have the same passion for your marketing materials. A great first impression leads your target audience to contact you, whether it's by e-mail, phone, or your website. Great first impressions with your marketing materials bring you more business. Hunter John Designs makes great first impressions with your business.

Now, to break that down: I grab your attention by saying that I make you look good. We all think about how we are perceived by others. We want to give a great first impression, and we should have those same concerns about our marketing materials.

I also tell you, "A great first impression leads your target audience to contact you, whether it's by e-mail, phone, or your website." Everyone wants new business. My design creates an accurate message for your business. When your introduction is clear, consistent, and accurate, the target audience will contact you. Then it's up to the prospective client to take it from there. We as designers have done our part by creating an accurate message that compels the client to take action. Just in those few sentences of introduction, I have created a sizzle to grab their attention and make them want more information after the meeting.

This process is constantly changing. I try to mix it up. I force myself out of my comfort zone and think outside the box. I listen to other introductions to see what works and what doesn't. I test it out on my friends or colleagues to get their opinion.

Don't be afraid to mix it up too. You want to grab a person's attention. You don't want to sound like a robot that didn't put much thought into the introduction. It is much like going for an interview. You study your answers because you want to sound confident. Well, it takes the same level of seriousness and commitment to have a great introduction. If you appear nervous, you won't seem confident with your material—and you want to sound like an expert in your field. As you attend different networking meetings, you will notice that many people don't seem prepared and are saying "um" a lot. You don't want to sound unprofessional or, even worse, sound like you don't know what you are talking about.

SAMPLE INTRODUCTION 2

I'm Lisa Polce of Hunter John Designs. I bring to the table twenty years of experience in the graphic design industry. We make sure that you have great marketing materials with a consistent, accurate message to your target audience. We bring your message to life using the elements of graphic design: logos, color, text, fonts, white space, photography, or computer-generated images. We don't necessarily use all these elements, but rather select ones which will be best for your message. Contact Hunter John Designs to help with your next project.

It can also benefit yourself to show ways you look out for other businesses as part of your networking travels. Remember that networking is planting seeds—helping others in order to help yourself.

SAMPLE INTRODUCTION 3

I was in Staples picking up some office supplies. Two employees happened to be having a conversation about needing a florist. I was next up to pay for my items. I thought to myself, *Should I say something?* Then I thought, *Sure, why not?* I said, "I don't mean to eavesdrop on your conversation, but do you need a florist?" The clerk replied yes, so I said, "A good friend of mine and colleague is a florist. I have her number on my phone." I spoke very highly of her and suggested that the clerk call her. The clerk asked for her number, and I gave it to her. Her grandmother had died, and she wanted to send some flowers.

The clerk did contact my friend for flowers, and it ended up being a $300 order. Now, $300 isn't earth-shattering, but it's an order just the same, and one she probably wouldn't have had if I hadn't spoken up. This is a great example of using listening skills and constantly thinking of how you can generate business for others.

Thank-You Notes

Your marketing also needs to include sending thank-you notes. It sounds so simple, but not many people do it. I'm not talking about a text, an e-mail, or a phone call; I'm talking about a good, old-fashioned card in the mail. If I had to give out one of my secrets, it is this part of my marketing. I send thank-you notes. I send them for coffees, for business, for sending a referral, or just to say "nice to meet you." Making people feel appreciated goes a long way in this world. Remember how you felt the last time someone went out of his or her way to appreciate you.

I also try to send a "keep in touch" card. Every once in a while, just touch base with your customers or clients. It's part of running a business, and it should be a part of your customer service. With technology advancing and with instant contact becoming the norm, a thank-you note makes you stand out and be remembered.

Your Website

I planned to have my website go live within six months. Thinking about a website can get overwhelming. There are so many aspects of a designer's site. My advice here is to think of yours as an online portfolio to help market your business. I didn't want a lot of pages, because the most important characteristics to me were simplicity, organization, and user-friendliness. You don't want your visitors to be confused. Because we are designers, we must remind ourselves sometimes that simple is better and less is more. Don't have so much going on that your website looks too busy.

What Do You Want from Your Website?

Get out a piece of paper and start writing down what you want on your website:

Headers

Tabs

Graphics

Samples

Testimonials

Contact info

Slide show

Your service categories

What makes you different

What you include on your website will depend on your taste, what you want to convey, and what your budget will allow. Depending on your budget and skill set, you may opt to design your own site. This will save you money, which is always good. Honestly speaking, my interests do not cover coding, hosting, HTML, or Web development. I outsourced that part of my website to one of my colleagues, Jim Smith, coauthor of this book and author of *How to Start a Home-based Web Design Business*. Nice to have someone like that in my corner.

A business website is a reflection of your business and the message you are trying to convey. It is also a marketing tool that you will use to get new business. If you are not designing your own website, I would advise hiring someone who understands the search engine optimization (SEO) aspect of Web development. You can have the coolest website, but if people can't find you, what good is it? The developer you hire should also offer hosting and have great customer service. Make sure the person does not have downtime and will be available to keep up with your website changes as needed.

You don't have to follow in my footsteps and wait a year before creating a website. In fact, I would advise against making the same mistake I made. You should try to have your website launch coincide with the opening of your business.

Now, website design is not just about looks. Yes, we are designers, but we have to take on the daunting task of writing our content, too. Be a perfectionist—don't have spelling or grammar errors. It looks unprofessional. When writing content, keep in mind your audience and speak to them in words they can understand. Your prospective clients may not know what four-color process and RGB mean, or what bleeds do.

HOW I CHOSE MY URL

The name of my business is Hunter John Designs, LLC. If I used the name of the business as my URL—well, that could mean anything. It could mean interior design, general contracting, home design, or bathroom remodeling. You get my point. When it came to the URL for my business website, I wanted to have the words "graphic design" in the address and also keep Hunter John in the name somehow. I came up with www.hjgraphicdesigns.com—HJ being my company's initials and the keywords "graphic designs." Thus, my URL was born. Be savvy with your URL name. If you can, try to use a dot-com name rather than dot-net or dot-biz. A dot-com name indicates a stable business that has been around for a while.

Another website area you should think about is accomplishments. When you own your own business, you also have to do your own public relations. Pat yourself on the back, because no one else will. If you are quoted in an article or get some press time, share the link on your website. If you have won an award or obtained certification, say it or even take a picture of it. It adds to your credibility.

I find it hard to bring attention to myself. I get the feeling that I am bragging or sounding overconfident. But if we were associated with an advertising firm and it won an award, I would bet that its public relations department would send out a press release announcing the great news. If anything happens to you that will bring good publicity, by all means share it. Send the information to the local papers. Of course, it is up to them to print the information, but you can always try. Whether it is an award, presentation, certificate, or a donation to charity, don't be afraid to spread the word about your good fortune if it will put your design business in the spotlight.

HOW I DESIGNED MY WEBSITE

Home Page
When I did my website, I did it in pieces. First I wrote the home page, which can be a simple welcome message thanking people for visiting your site, or you can share what services you have to offer.

About Us
The "About Us" page was a little more personal. I told my story and talked about my experience.

Portfolio
This section shares some of my samples and explains the purpose and results. I wanted my website to be simple, not complicated, so I kept my website's portfolio simple as well. Agonizing over which sample to use took the most time. I like all my work, so I spent a lot of time on this part of the site.

Testimonials
I think featuring people who have vouched for your work is necessary on any home-based business website. Here is some commonsense advice for testimonials: Don't make them up. Have clients send you their testimonials and always ask permission to use them. If a client has sent an e-mail to you or called you with some kind words that would sound good as a testimonial, simply send that person a reply e-mail thanking him or her for the nice comment and asking if it

(continued on next page)

(continued from previous page)

would be okay to run the testimonial on your website. Most people will not only agree to it, but they will be delighted that you appreciated their opinion enough to share it with others.

On my website, I made sure I got a good mixture of testimonials for various services I offer. For example, I used an image of a brochure with one testimonial. I had some kind words from a trade show client for a flyer I designed, and I put in a testimonial from a client I helped who was up against a tight deadline. It is best to show a nice variety of your services and skills.

Contact Us

As important as your portfolio is, so is how people contact you. Make sure to include your e-mail and phone number so that prospective clients have different ways to reach you. You can include your home address for mail if you want or give it directly when requested if you don't feel comfortable posting it on your website.

As I write this, I am thinking about revisiting my website, no pun intended, to give it a fresh look. Keep in mind that you need to spend time working on your website, so use your time wisely. This is where you need to balance spending time on your business and spending time on what brings in your immediate income, your design time. Although having a great website will bring you business, putting it together definitely requires a balancing act with your other tasks. For instance, I have been putting aside time to write this book, to meet deadlines, and to keep up with my client workload. Stay organized and prioritize.

Don't forget that your website is a necessary tool for your business. Take time to do it and do it right. You don't need to have all kinds of pages, Adobe Flash–driven graphics, music, or any other bells and whistles. If you are great at Web design, all the better, but some of us designers are not. Remember that what drives people to your site is your *content*. When I was writing my content, I showed it to some colleagues and had them critique it for me. I am my own worst critic and really hard on myself, so I had to step back a little. Most of the time, the feedback is something as simple as just tweaking some of the wording.

Speaking from experience, I would suggest writing one page at a time. Just remember that your website can be tweaked, changed, and given a fresh look over time—so if it isn't perfect, do the best you can and get it up there to let it gel for a while. Something is better than nothing, and you can always make changes down the road.

The Advantages of a Website

One thing to keep in mind is that while you physically have a home office location, with limitations on the hours you are open and closed, the Internet is open 24 hours a day, 7 days a week, 365 days a year. It never closes, so your website does not close either. It's kind of cool to think about—because the Internet never closes, you can get a new client anytime.

Another advantage to having a website is that it's usually cheaper and less expensive than creating a lot of print material. Now, don't get me wrong—we need print material to market ourselves, but having something electronic, like a website, allows us to make changes and revisions at a low cost.

While I'm on advantages of a website, this next one can be a disadvantage as well. You can be anywhere in the world and still gain business from different regions because of your website. Although you can do business in your local market, you can also be active all over the country and have clients anywhere. A website provides global reach. This can be good and bad: good because you can have clients everywhere, bad because some of us like to give back to the community and do business locally. There is a trend to shop local. I certainly wouldn't turn away new clients because they are in another town, state, or country, but there is something I like about helping a local business get off the ground and giving back. Just doing business in my hometown gives me a great sense of accomplishment. Remember how you started. It is nice to have a local businessperson support your business.

Business on the Internet can happen instantaneously. If someone visits your site and you have what that person needs, he or she will most likely contact you. One of the perks of having a website is that it brings legitimacy and credibility to your business.

When I am shopping for something and I want more information on the product, I will most likely use the Internet. When I am visiting other sites, I find that I don't have a lot of confidence in a company if its website doesn't look right. What I mean by this is whether or not the website will meet my needs. Is it user-friendly?

Are there so many links or pages to click on that it gets confusing to the point where I lose interest and leave the site? Be thinking of these aspects when designing your website.

A company website can instill confidence and give the appearance that your business is bigger than it actually is. Maybe you are a one-person show, but you don't necessarily want that to come across on your website. You know your trade and have the skills to do a great job. Your colleagues are part of your arsenal and can offer various resources, such as a copywriter, photographer, Web developer, social media guru, commercial printer, etc. You get the idea. You may also have the additional resource of partners or staff. Either way, as you grow, your website can grow, too. Above all else, a website needs to be fresh and current. It is an ongoing marketing tool that needs to be tweaked as your business develops.

One last thing I want to caution you about: Be prompt about getting back to customers who contact you through your website. You know how frustrating it can be when you have to wait for information when contemplating a purchase or decision and the website people don't get back to you. Don't do that to your website visitors. Get back to your potential client in a timely manner.

Social Media Marketing

As I have mentioned throughout the book, technology is moving at lightning speed. Just when you feel you are caught up, someone comes up with the latest trend, newest gadget, or faster way to improve on your bottom line and business. As business owners, we have a mindset that we need to adjust to this ever-quickening pace of the digital information.

This leads me to social media. Social media has really come of age over the past few years. It has become an iconic way of sharing information, conversation, photos, charity causes, and tidbits about life, and, for the business world, a way of attracting a bigger and wider audience. This range of opportunities certainly wasn't possible through more traditional marketing methods in the past.

Facebook

I finally started using Facebook personally a few years ago. It intrigued me to see what everyone was talking about, and it was great to connect with high school and college friends. I became a frequent user on my personal page. However, even though I enjoyed connecting with old friends and sharing photos of family, I wasn't keen on using it for my business at first. It wasn't until about six months later that I decided to make a business Facebook page.

In my opinion, a Facebook business page is just that—for business only. There can be a fine line between your business page and your personal page. Keep them separate, and don't post anything personal on your business page. It may sound obvious, but I've seen people frequently use their personal page for business and vice versa. Avoid doing this. My business page is for business networking and posts related to my business or industry. You should view yours as an extension of your website and marketing. Use it in the proper way.

My business page features my logo, showcases my projects, and gives my clients the spotlight as well. It is, for all practical purposes, free advertising. It is an opportunity to publicize your business accolades and a chance to share business-oriented tips, news, or other information that might be relevant.

A word of caution: Make sure you read Facebook's rules and regulations for business pages. I do not talk about price or competitors, nor do I post anything that sounds like I'm selling my services. For instance, I might post some networking tips or five steps to designing a great logo, or simply wish my clients a good weekend. I do not say, "Need graphic design? Call Hunter John Designs." There is a time and place for everything, and Facebook or any social media site is not the place to be obnoxious.

Facebook uses "Likes" on your business page, just as on your personal page. Everyone is into numbers. I would appreciate more "Likes" on my business page, but I don't want to artificially inflate that number and have just anyone liking my page. Then those numbers wouldn't mean anything, and my visitors would quickly figure that out.

Another good use for your Facebook business page is to post a recent tip or alert for your customers. When you post relevant industry information, it adds to your credibility as an expert in your field. People will begin to trust your expertise.

When I use the Hunter John Designs Facebook page, it's an extension of my business. You should handle your page in a professional manner. There is a fine line between sounding cocky versus displaying your knowledge as an expert. You can show links to industry-related blogs. If you hear a good quote or learn something new, by all means, share it. I try to share posts about organizations that I am involved with, such as the local chamber, the Advertising Club of Connecticut, and BNI.

Another good tip for using Facebook or any social media site is to have their icons (Facebook, LinkedIn, Twitter, etc.) on your website and in your e-mail signature. Likewise, post your website on your social media accounts as live links. Traffic going to your website, as well as to your social media keeps your business active and builds good website traffic through higher rankings in the search engines. Traffic to your website creates an increase in traffic to your website? Yes, search engines track the activity of websites to determine which ones warrant higher listings—thus increased traffic.

Facebook is a fun way to stay connected with your clients. Once you create a post and people respond to it, it gives you exposure to countless people and, more important, a possible new client base. I see people all the time post for services they need—for example, "I need a painter. Anyone know a good interior painter?" or "I need a professional photographer for some product photos. Please message me with some names you recommend." You can easily seize the opportunity that Facebook presents to build your network of business owners.

Twitter

If you have an event and you want to create some buzz, consider using Twitter. Talk about fast. You can't get any faster than Twitter. It is a network that connects users to the most current news and events. If it's happening out there in the world, you will hear about it on Twitter.

Twitter, like other social media, keeps you connected to your existing customers and potential customers. It works for businesses as long as your "followers" on Twitter are interested in your products or services. It is certainly a growing phenomenon for people to see or hear about world events (or your products) and tweet their thoughts. This lends itself well to the business world. The trends are out there, and some are here to stay.

LinkedIn

I was using LinkedIn as a business owner long before I joined Facebook. LinkedIn is geared much more toward business professionals. You should utilize the profile feature on other social media sites, but especially on LinkedIn to get your business information out there to the business world.

LinkedIn is basically the go-to networking site for business professionals all over the world. Professionals use it to promote their businesses, look for jobs, set up business ventures, and establish and further their reputations in their fields. It allows you to create a profile and add a head shot, and it displays your information in an organized manner. So create a LinkedIn profile, add your website link, and list your other credentials. Clients and colleagues can recommend your services, and you can recommend your clients and colleagues in return.

LinkedIn has grown exponentially in the past few years. Today there are hundreds of millions of users. The site offers the business world at your fingertips, and the opportunities for meeting new colleagues, clients, and customers are endless.

LinkedIn is successful because it's user-friendly and, for the basic services, free to use. The profiles are easy to set up and easy to edit. Over time, you will make more and more professional connections via LinkedIn and other social media sites.

Just like everything else, be careful who you connect to. You should at least know the person. Some people are out there for the quantity (i.e., "How many connections can I get?"), just like Facebook. It's really about building relationships, staying connected, and keeping up with industry or business trends.

LinkedIn is certainly geared toward business, networking, and professional contacts, but you can also post or blog about something you learned or can get the word out about an event. There are a lot of insightful posts, most of which are not about the person posting but someone sharing information.

LinkedIn's reach is powerful. It can bring you connections from all over the world. With that kind of reach, it becomes a great marketing tool.

Putting It All Together

When you organize a noteworthy event, you may find that you want to post it on Facebook, LinkedIn, Twitter, and possibly other sites. There is a nice program on the Internet called Composer (composer.io) that allows you to post your news and select which of your social media sites you want to publish to. Then it automatically sends it to all of them for you. I don't recommend going crazy posting insignificant items just to keep your name in front of everyone. But it won't hurt to put something informative out there once a week or, at the most, once a day for any of your followers to enjoy.

Social media seems to have left its mark on the business world and is making leaps and bounds toward becoming part of our daily agenda. Companies are growing, and with that growth comes change. We need to adapt to marketing our businesses in the lightning-fast world of online marketing.

The old-fashioned marketing methods are by no means obsolete, though. Meeting face-to-face, shaking people's hands, and looking them in the eye all go a long way in establishing a client relationship. But the digital world has definitely entered our marketplace. We need to keep up with the trends of our industry.

Using social media, like having a website, has gained its place in the business plan. Make it work for you. I have more and more clients asking me to add social media icons to their marketing materials. The general public wants to know that businesses are on top of these trends. There are businesses that offer social media coaching. Reach out to them to understand all that these sites can do for you, your clients, and your business.

Social media has a place in your business, so I encourage you to add it to your marketing arsenal and have fun with it. Always use it professionally and appropriately. It is, after all, your reputation and integrity on the line. All situations and business philosophies are different, so develop your own style and social media will help your business grow.

The Internet

As a Graphic Designer, Should You Be a Web Designer, Too?

Because this book is coauthored by a graphic designer and a Web designer, we have some strong opinions on the crossover between graphic design and Web design. Some Web designers are excellent graphic designers, but most are not. Some graphic designers are excellent Web designers, but most are not. Why is there such a divide between the two?

Most Web designers are actually Web developers—they are generally "designers" in name only. Web designers tend to be technically focused instead of artistic. Most are very happy to try to create nice-looking pages behind the scenes using HTML code.

Graphic designers who create websites typically use a WYSIWYG (What You See Is What You Get) program to develop websites. They are more focused on how the website looks than on getting that last bit of coding cleaned up.

You may be one of the rare graphic designers who not only creates good designs, but also loves to go into the HTML code and CSS style sheets to tweak and perfect them. But most graphic designers who think they are great at Web design really are not, and most Web designers who think they hold the key to great design really are not that amazing.

You can be a great Web designer and fairly good graphic designer and get away with using some attractive templates so that you can offer both services. And as a great graphic designer, you can usually master some powerful Web design tools so that you can provide a good product.

Hooking Up with a Web Designer

Rather than spending your time and talents trying to keep up with the ever-changing field of Web design, consider making a connection with a few good

Web designers. It might take you a while to find the right match, but it will be worth it. Eventually you will find a Web designer who does not like dealing with the mundane task of finding the right color blends for a website. You will find a Web designer who loves to tweak the code so your artwork is not only well displayed, but also structured well for the Internet.

A good Web designer should be able to teach you some basics of website layout while not thwarting your design efforts. In other words, there may be some sound reasons for a Web designer to request that you design a site with the navigation menu across the top instead of down the left side, or vice versa. You will need to find a Web designer who works well with you as a team member and not one who just has a set idea of how a website should look without considering your thoughts on the design. Flexibility on both sides should result in a great-looking *and* functional website.

So how do you know what makes a good Web designer? A good one should be well versed in appealing to the search engines. If you work with a designer who takes your design work and puts the entire graphic into the homepage, there is no text on that critical homepage for search engines to see. A quick test you can do is to highlight a webpage (in Windows, CTRL-A will highlight all text), copy that page, open a text editor such as Notepad, and paste the page into the text editor. If little or no text shows up from that webpage, that is what the search engines will see as well. They can't read your graphics; they rely on text to see what to catalog.

A red flag is if the Web developer puts a note on the website that it is best viewed in a certain browser (Firefox, Internet Explorer, Chrome, etc.). Your Web designer should be able to take your designs and rework them into a fully functional website that looks good on all modern browsers and computers. If he or she develops it on a PC and on your Mac it looks nothing like you expected (words hidden behind images, sections rearranged, etc.), it needs to be fixed. If the designer can't fix it, you don't want your reputation tied to his or her work.

Check any changes on various screen sizes. If the designer uses a standard screen size such as 1024 x 768 pixels, try looking at it on a wide screen. Try reducing the size of the screen to half its current size. Ideally it should look good either way. It may not look the same as it gets smaller, but the text certainly should not slip behind the images, nor should the text get scrunched together in a narrow column a few characters wide.

It is not easy to create a website with that kind of flexibility. The more creative you are in the design, the harder it is to match your ideas to a good website. But if the Web designer you are working with has more excuses than talents, it might be time to find someone better suited to please your clients.

The Future of the Internet

If only we could peek into the future. At the time of writing this book, desktop PC usage is starting to decline. Laptops, tablets, and smartphones are taking away some of that market. Now websites need to not only look good on large screens, but also be functional and look good on iPhones and other handheld mobile devices. It is important to stay on top of the trends.

You may find a market opening up to transform a large website into a small website for mobile phones. On a desktop, your restaurateur-client might feel it is most important for you to design their website to get the visitor to view the menus or use an online reservation system. However, if visitors are looking for a restaurant on their mobile phones, the restaurant owner may have some studies that indicate that the visitor likely just wants a big button to "Call Us" and one to "Find Us" because they are already interested and just need directions on their phone or want to call ahead for reservations. As the restaurant's graphic designer, you need to make that limited space as attractive and useful as possible. If you keep on top of user trends like this, you may be able to pick up on some new business that your competitors have not gotten up to speed on yet.

Should a Graphic Designer Offer Social Media?

Social media is still a developing and changing part of Internet services. You may have clients asking you to create a Facebook design or other social media designs. If you feel comfortable installing your designs into the applications, it might be a nice way to get your foot in the door so that you can get more business from a new client. Or find someone with those skills to work with you and translate your designs into online showpieces.

This is a good time to mention that if you can respond to your clients in a meaningful way on questions like this, you are going to become the go-to guru for a lot of their queries. That is one of the reasons I like involving other business pros on my informal team. If a client has a question about social media matters, I know someone who loves to tinker in that. She is a great resource and knows that if she helps my clients, I'm willing to share my clients in areas that can benefit both of us. Just make sure your social media gurus (or Web designer or others) understand that you will not tolerate their taking your clients away. If they do that once, it will be the last client you ever share with them.

Coauthor Jim Smith worked with another graphic designer before he met me. He had her work on a website design for a client, only to find out from the client that she was conducting a smear campaign against him to the client. She ultimately convinced that client to have another friend of hers take care of the website. Jim confronted the client and learned that some untruths had been said. Naturally, that was the last job she got from Jim. Treat your circle of professionals respectfully and make sure they understand that the arrangement should work for everyone involved.

Appendix A: Website Resources

Here I listed websites that have been mentioned in this book or that I think will be valuable to you. This list is presented for convenience and is by no means exhaustive.

Change This
(changethis.com)
This website consists of quality, well-written articles. Most are geared toward small marketing and graphic design businesses. For a good starting point, find the article on "The Design Funnel" by Stephen Hay.

COLOURLovers
(colourlovers.com)
Here is a wonderful site with everything you'd ever want to know about colors—how to blend them, how to use them, even which colors to use in your themes. The site has color palettes, articles, tips, and more.

Fotolia
(fotolia.com)
Fotolia is similar to iStock Photo, but I find some of the prices to be better. They offer a full range of images, videos, and some vector art.

Graphic Designers at Home
(homebaseddesigner.com)
This website is an addendum to this book **put together by the authors.** It contains additional articles and tips shared by the authors and others in the industry. Stop by and share your own tips or ideas.

Iconfinder

(iconfinder.com)

This site is handy if you are looking for ideas for representational icon art for your project. Search for "Twitter" if you want to see an example of some of the creative icons available.

iStock Photo

(istockphoto.com)

Here you will find photography, video, illustrations, and audio that are supplied by industry professionals. Buy credits to obtain the rights to use the material.

VectorStock

(vectorstock.com)

Vector images on this site can be easily expanded and reduced in size due to their structure. VectorStock is similar to iStock Photo but for vector images. You can buy credits to use these images.

You the Designer

(youthedesigner.com)

This website is full of good articles and tips for graphic designers. Look for the article "How Designers Use Color to Influence Consumers" as a good starting point.

Appendix B: Organizations

American Institute of the Graphic Arts (AIGA)
(aiga.org)
AIGA was established in 1914. With over twenty thousand members, it is the largest membership-driven professional association for graphic design.

Art Directors Club (ADC)
(adcglobal.org)
The Art Directors Club has been around since 1920. The club offers various programs, awards, and educational opportunities, including student scholarships.

Business Network International (BNI)
(bni.com)
This organization helps generate business through structured word-of-mouth referrals. The organization focuses on building relationships and truly helping others succeed. Visit the website to find your local chapter.

Chamber Groups
Join the chamber of commerce in your town to kick-start your local networking.

Graphic Artists Guild
(graphicartistsguild.org)
The Graphic Artists Guild, founded in 1967, has six regional chapters throughout the United States. It is well known for its excellent reference book, *The Graphic Artists Guild Handbook: Pricing & Ethical Guidelines*, for graphic designers.

International Council of Graphic Design Associations (ICOGRADA)

(icograda.org)

ICOGRADA is an international graphic design organization active in over sixty countries worldwide.

Meetup Meetings

(meetup.com)

Search for a graphic design meeting in your vicinity or a business networking meeting nearby. If there is nothing available, perhaps you should try to start one. Meetup listings are a great way to get to know like-minded individuals in your area.

National Association of Photoshop Professionals (NAPP)

(photoshopuser.com)

If you are a fan of Adobe's Photoshop graphic editor, you might want to think about joining the NAPP. This is an organization whose focus is on offering tutorials and tips for Photoshop users.

Appendix C: Educational Resources and Training Programs

I would highly recommend attending a college or university that offers graphic design as a degree program. The training begins with you and what you studied in college. When I went to college, which wasn't very long ago, the university I attended had Introduction to Graphics 101, 102, etc. It didn't even offer a graphic design curriculum or graphic design major. I took courses that were very basic, nowhere near at the level offered today at many major universities. If college isn't for you, I highly recommend learning the Adobe Creative Suite programs inside and out. Learn as much as you can from the literature, and learn even more when you start working in the programs. These applications are constantly changing. You need to stay on top of the current trends.

Adobe.com

The official Adobe website is full of information about Adobe products and has an extensive training and tutorial section.

Lynda.com

This tutorial website offers videos and webinars on software, business topics, and creative skills. The training follows up-to-date trends and is recognized throughout much of the creative industry.

Psdtuts+

(psd.tutsplus.com)
Psdtuts+ is a collection of top-notch Photoshop tutorials, articles, tips, and even video training clips.

Typophile

(typophile.com)

Whether you occasionally manipulate fonts in your works or are a typography-focused graphic designer, take advantage of Typophile's extensive blog, forum, and wealth of information on typography.

Job

Update the existing double-sided, two-page office brochure with use of photos, fonts, stock photography, text, and corporate colors.

Purpose

Client wants to update and improve the look of the office brochure. The design has to use existing corporate colors, and the brochure must remain the same size.

Process

The first step was to meet with the client. It's really important to meet with clients to get to know them, but it's even more important to listen to what they want to accomplish. The client and I talked about colors, use of professional photography, photos of the doctor's office, the text supplied, use of the logo, and the general feel of the brochure. The client was open to filtering in stock photography. We talked about text, use of the logo, and how to present the information in a professional way. It was important to the client to stay consistent with the colors throughout the brochure. I took notes, gathered information, and then considered all the pieces that had to come together to reach our goal of a great updated brochure. The tedious part was coming up with a price that would be comfortable for the both of us.

Hint: Really think of yourself as a professional. You are worth it. Don't undervalue yourself. On the other hand, don't overcharge either. It's a very delicate balance when it comes to quoting on a project. You need to make money, and the client needs to think it's a fair price. Designing is very personal.

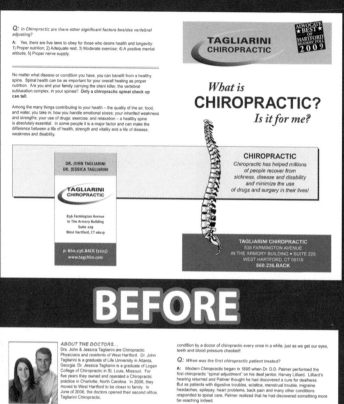

The before and after, although in black-and-white, shows how we used the professional photos, stock photography, logo, fonts, text, white space, and teamwork, which I call the "elements of design."

use of:

logos
colors
graphics
white space
text
teamwork

AFTER

Hunter John Designs, llc

As a designer you can spend hours just going over fonts or colors. Always remember that your time is valuable and that you are a professional.

The client had an existing brochure. I reached out to the previous designer and asked to have the files forwarded to me. Although this provided a good base and made it easier to handle the text (which the client edited, anyway), I really stripped the brochure down to nothing and redesigned it.

At Hunter John Designs, we try to submit a proof that is practically flawless. No, it doesn't have to be perfect, but we really scrutinize the layout, use of color, white space, photography, placement of photography, and fonts. There are other things you need to pay attention to as well, but these are some of the important ones. It's really important to print and mock up your proof, even if the design looks great on screen. Cut it out and spray-mount it together. Determine how it folds and how the text appears with the fold. Even after doing graphic design as long as I have, I always see something that can be moved or nudged away from the fold. It seems like common sense in the design world, but you would be surprised how many people don't take the time to look over a proof before they send it to a client.

I designed the layout with the appropriate pieces of the puzzle: photos used near text that was relevant to the topic being presented. We took into consideration proper use of the logo and corporate colors. With every project, I implement the "elements of design" to bring the project to life. In the instance of the doctor's office brochure, I asked myself whether it was something I would read. Would I keep it or tell someone about it if the need arose?

I am proud of my work. You have to take pride in your work, because it will be something that showcases your skills to the public. You want to make it interesting enough to catch the eye and easy to read, and you should include information that someone will keep instead of throw away.

Throughout the project, there were revisions, but in the end, we both had a great brochure. I was happy with the design, and the client was happy with the brochure. Last but not least, once we had a final proof and we were ready to submit the file to a printer, the client and I talked about the choice of paper that would be best suited for the design. Great design is important, and so is the correct choice of paper and commercial printer. If you have to, get a sample of the paper. Touch it, feel it. Is it appropriate for the project? Sometimes it even helps when you can get a printed sample on the paper you want to use. I'm lucky to have had prepress experience in my career. I can pass that knowledge on to my clients.

It's really important in the graphic design industry to understand how something will look printed and how to submit your files to get printed. Get to know several printers, and be loyal to them. They become strong colleagues and partners who are there to help when you need them.

Index

insurance, 68–69
invoices, 89–91
money, keeping track of, 93–94
photos, 81
plan for, 45–49
pricing goods and services, 70–73
quotes, 83–86
status and desires, 40
five Ws, in press releases, 113
flat fees, 71–72, 73
free, working for, 78–80
freelancing, 13, 55, 56. *See also* self-employment
FreshBooks, 89, 91
furniture, 27–28
future, long-term, 20–21
future services, 42

G
getting started
  brand identity, 57
  business goals/objectives, 60–64
  business identity, 58–59
  finances, 45–46, 66
  logo, 59–60, 61
  naming your business, 56–57
  operating expenses worksheet, 66
  planning stages, 53–56
  steps to opening your business, 64–65
  website, 64
goals, 40, 60–62, 63–64
graphic design market, 42–43
graphic design services, 17–20, 41–42

hard drives, external, 30
home office
  business plan description, 51
  checklist, 24
  computer, 24, 28–31
  equipment and tools, 24, 28–35
  furniture, 27–28
  Internet and e-mail browser, 34
  lighting, 35
  location, 23, 25–27
  music, 35

phone, 35
printers, 24, 32–33
software applications, 24, 31–32
supplies, 35
honesty, 11
hourly rates, 70–71
human resources plan, 49

I
identity, business, 58–59
illustration, 17
improvement, 14–15
independent contractors, 104
independently, working, 5, 8
industrial design, 18
informational design, 18
insurance, 68–69
Internet
  browsers for, 34
  future of, 135
  social media, offering, 135–36
  Web design, offering, 133
  Web designers, hooking up with, 133–35
introducing your business, 120–22
invoices, 89–91

L
land lines, 35
laptops, 29
late fees, 87, 91
lawyers, 98, 99–100
layout, 19
legal and ethical issues
  attorneys, 98, 99–100
  business structure, 100–102
  contracts, legalities of, 102–5
  copyright issues, 105–10
liabilities, past, 97
lighting, 35
limited liability corporations (LLCs), 50, 101–2
LinkedIn, 130–31
location, 23, 25–27
logo design, 19, 59–60, 61